D1230623

THE GERBER REPORT

THE GERBER REPORT

The Shocking State of American Medical
Care and What Must Be
Done About It

by ALEX GERBER, M.D., F.A.C.S.

DAVID McKAY COMPANY, INC.

New York

THE GERBER REPORT

Second Printing, May 1971

To Rosalie, for her love and constant encourage-ment during the writing of this book.

ACKNOWLEDGMENTS

Various parts of this manuscript have been reviewed, and constructive suggestions made, by Dr. Sherman Mellinkoff, Dr. Keith Russell, Dr. Irving Benglesdorf, Roland Berg, and Richard Jones. I appreciate their help and support.

I am especially grateful to Dr. Roy Perkins for his critical comments on several key chapters. His unsurpassed knowledge of medical socioeconomics has been invaluable.

I am also greatly indebted to Jay Nelson Tuck for his editorial assistance.

Finally, my thanks to William White, editor of *Family Health*, for his encouraging review of my manuscript.

Alex Gerber, M.D.

South Pasadena, Calif.

CONTENTS

THE GERBER REPORT

1

WHAT'S WRONG—AND RIGHT—
ABOUT AMERICAN MEDICINE

IN a comfortable bed in a modern, sunny room in a fully accredited hospital lies Mrs. Molly Jones, who has just had her uterus removed. The service is good, the nurses are cheerful and helpful, and her doctor is most solicitous of her feelings and welfare. The Jones family has no money, so Mrs. Jones's care will be paid for by Medicaid. Only a few years ago she would have had to go to the despised county hospital. Now she is getting "mainstream" medical care, the same that would be rendered to anyone who could pay.

On the floor below Mrs. Jones in the immaculate, bustling, pediatric section of the hospital is little Tommy Brown, who has just surrendered his tonsils. Tommy's family has no money either, yet he too is receiving mainstream care. The stigma of charity medicine is gone. It is indeed a happy picture.

Or is it? It might be except for one disturbing fact: *neither Mrs. Jones nor little Tommy needed the operation.* Mrs. Jones's uterus and Tommy's tonsils were perfectly healthy. Both patients have undergone unnecessary pain and suffering, in each case at some risk of life. Each is worse off than he was before, at least to that extent. Both occupy beds that are needed by seriously ill patients. The taxpayers will have paid out sizable sums that were totally wasted. The only persons who benefit are the doctors who collect fees for having performed the operations.

You may think that this is an exceptional incident. It is not. It occurs hundreds of times in this country every day. These unnecessary operations are but one example among many of where our health care has gone terribly, terribly wrong. Health care in the United States is a crazy patchwork of some of the world's best medicine and some practices that would disgrace a folk operator in Lower Patagonia.

Can't something be done to prevent the kind of mayhem to which Mrs. Jones and Tommy were subjected? Surely there are plenty of people with the power to put an end to such medical abuses. The trouble is that while the power is there, all too often no one is willing to exercise it. Neither organized medicine, Government agencies, nor health insurers will do anything to keep Mrs. Jones's uterus or Tommy's tonsils where they belong, rather than in formaldehyde on the pathologist's shelf. Dr. George James, dean of the Mount Sinai School of Medicine, was not entirely joking when he said, "The great thing about Medicare and Medicaid is that they now entitle a lot of old and poor people to the same poor quality of medical care that the rest of us get."

Yet for most health conscious Americans, this is the best of times. Diseases that would have killed or crippled us only a few years ago have been largely conquered now, or even, as in the case of polio, wiped out. New therapeutic procedures give many more years of productive life to thousands every year. Highly respected physicians and well-trained allied professionals work in modern, superbly equipped hospitals and offices. In 1970 we spent, from all sources, some $70 billion—7.0 percent of the gross national product—on our vital health services, less than we spent on alcohol, tobacco, and gambling. Despite the rapidly rising cost of health care, the public evidently believes that it is getting its money's worth. According to a recent Harris poll, a large majority of Americans are far more satisfied with the value received for their medical care dollars than with what they get when they buy food, clothing, and shelter.

For other Americans it is the worst of times. The fabric of our medical care is of uneven texture. The health statistics of the American poor more closely resemble the statistics of Tanzania than they do the glowing record of more affluent and knowledgeable Americans. Many people are often not treated at all, and when they are treated, it may be not by the skilled and well trained, but by the unqualified, the commercial operators, the semi-charlatans or the outright quacks. Usually they cannot afford good quality care; often they are too timid or too uninformed to seek it; often they do not know the difference between good and bad. For them the bright image of Marcus Welby, MD, comes from the television screen in a cloud of visual static.

There is our dilemma: How are we to elevate the health level of these millions of medically disadvantaged to the level enjoyed by their more fortunate neighbors? Their level is so low that they drag down our national statistics far below those of other industrial countries, as reported by the World Health Organization. The United

States ranks eighteenth among nations in infant mortality, twenty-second in longevity. Surely this is a paradox! The United States leads the world in industrial production, in the wizardry of our weapons systems, and most certainly in the number of hospital-room TV sets. We are the richest and most powerful country on earth. Why are we not the healthiest?

There are those who put our problem in terms of a crisis bordering on the catastrophic and who predict an "Armageddon for the medical profession." There are respected authorities who look for nothing short of a revolution in medicine that in its effects will rival the industrial revolution or the scientific upheaval created by the transition from Ptolemaic to Copernican astronomy. The more violent of the demolition experts among the radical young would leave no bastion of the status quo unblasted, starting with the medical schools. One of them gave his answer to the imperfections of medical education: "to destroy the medical schools, to destroy them completely."

Skipping such rhetoric, but granting the seriousness of the quandary, how are our various power blocs responding to the very real problem? How are we to reconcile the disparate views of the American Medical Association, the American Hospital Association, the Association of American Medical Colleges, the American Academy of General Practice, the specialty boards, Federal health officials, congressmen, labor unions, consumer groups, the health foundations, and the Young Lords?

There is certainly no shortage of talk about the matter. Every phase of health care comes under the scrutiny of a constant procession of blue-ribbon commissions, White House task forces, think tanks, and congressional committees. There is an endless series of meetings at which the medical elite present their analyses and propose solutions. Finally, the inevitable proclamation is issued from the Oval Room at the White House (during the summer, the action switches to the rose garden). They all agree that it is good to be in good health and bad to be in bad health, especially if you are poor. The deluge of reports and speeches adds little beyond prolixity to the summation of the problem made two generations ago by medical educator Dr. Willard Rappleye: "Probably the greatest problem confronting the medical profession at the present time is that of securing a *proper distribution* of *modern medical knowledge* to the *entire population* at *a reasonable cost*" (italics mine).

Whose fault is it that we are so little nearer that goal today than we were then? Most commonly the finger of blame is jabbed into those who are traditionally held responsible for the country's health—its doctors. We are faulted for being ill prepared, badly organized, and poorly motivated to "better the public health." This is a chicken that has come home to roost in the hen house of the American Medical Association. People are suspicious of organized medicine, saying that the AMA has bitterly resisted almost every forward movement in the last forty years. Yet it is interesting to note that most people speak with pride and affection of "my doctor," even though they may not like organized medicine.

The public clamors for changes in medical education, organization, service, and financing. Changes to what?

Medical schools, the starting point, are indicted for preparing "biological technicians" who are allegedly blind to the health needs of modern society. A rising chorus insists that the curriculum be changed to instill in the student a greater awareness of the sociological and economic problems that beset his patients. The torment of those espousing this philosophy was poignantly expressed by Dr. Jack Geiger of Tufts who condemned our schools for turning out physicians who "treat rat bites, but ignore the rats." The apostles of radical change envision the graduate of the future as a veritable Dr. Jack Armstrong, all-American boy, who will be not only medically competent, but also a quick-change artist able deftly to assume the roles of medical economist, social anthropologist, and urban planner as the moment demands.

Further, during the educational and training period, an increasing number of budding doctors is to be coaxed into adopting a new specialty, that of family physician. The almost moribund general practitioner is, like Lazarus, to be resurrected, glossed with several years of additional training, and rewarded for this added sheen by a change in title from GP to FP, duly certified by a framed parchment on the office wall. This new "family- and community-oriented" physician will not emulate the other "narrow" specialists, who allegedly treat diseases rather than people. Instead he will treat the whole person and be the "patient's advocate" within the medical system.

The medical school deans are caught in the middle of this curricular tug-of-war. On the one hand, they are prodded to add courses on the social sciences and humanities, including comparative religion, philosophy, and ethics, so that the new MD will more nearly approach the Renaissance man. On the other they are urged to stress more of the new scientific advances, such as those in molecular biology, immunology, and nuclear medicine. Some strongly advise greater emphasis on computerized medicine, systems analysis, and "biomedical engineering." At the same time, the dean must mediate between the traditional departments who want time to teach the core scientific and medical subjects. He must also cope with ever-increasing demands that the school give more community service and try to contend with the squabbles between "town and gown." Small wonder that the harassed medical school deans come and go with the monotonous frequency of professional football coaches. To the deans it must often seem that every season is a losing one. Their turnover rate in the 1960s was six times as great as it was during the 1950s. As Dr. Roger O. Egeberg, himself a dean at the University of Southern California at Los Angeles before he became assistant secretary of Health, Education and Welfare, put it, "A dean is to a medical school what a fire hydrant is to a dog."

The ferocious zeal of the reeducators is matched only by that of the reorganizers, who bemoan medicine's "fragmentation," "disorganization," and "staggering costs." They tell us that we are a "cottage industry" doing anachronistic "piecework," as though medical care were comparable to sewing buttons on a coat in a factory. The derisive epithet "nonsystem of health care"—or better, "an outmoded, Model T, nonsystem"—has been abused until it abrades the ear with rivet-hammer effect. What system of care will raise our health standards to those of Sweden, which has a homogeneous population and virtually no slums or unemployment?

The top health officials in Washington are especially convinced that medical practice must be restructured. Prepaid, closed-panel group clinics are being touted as the ultimate answer to our health-care problems. A special bureau exists within the Department of HEW just to promote such plans. And the department unveiled early in 1970 a proposal to add a new Part C to Medicare under which old people would go to such groups for preventive medicine, despite the fact that such groups exist only in a few large cities and would certainly be out of the reach of most people.

Washington also places a high priority on "increasing the doctor's productivity" by interposing between him and the nurse a new "physician's assistant." It is curious that the country with the world's highest living standard should be urged to accept such a person, while the Soviet Union hopes eventually to get rid of the *feldsher* (a health professional less than a doctor) and while Japan is rapidly phasing the *samba-san* (midwife) out of obstetrical care. If an American woman is assisted in delivery by a doctor, will her daughter be satisfied with a midwife?

Yet who can be complacent about the quality of medical care in this country? Only the most naive accept the oft-repeated AMA statements that our health care is "the finest in the world." The unhappy fact is that the recovery rate from war casualties is one of the few fields in which the United States can claim unquestioned preeminence. That outstanding record is matched by few of our civilian health statistics, some of which are strange indeed. Appendectomies are performed four times more frequently in southwestern Kansas than in some other parts of the state. Are the descendants of the rugged pioneers who settled Dodge City peculiarly less healthy than other Kansans? Or is there a more sinister explanation?

The Johnson Administration committed itself to achieve

universally distributed, high quality health care by law. A spate of health legislation poured through Congress during those hectic years. In a moment of refreshing candor, President Johnson acknowledged that the result of this *furor Americanus* was "a programmatic and bureaucratic nightmare." The nightmare is not over! Federal bureaucrats still continue to fragment health service through reorganizations.

Other authorities believe that quality care is to be bought rather than legislated into universal existence. The late Dr. Jack Masur, chief of the Clinical Center at the National Institutes of Health, said, "The pursuit of excellence in the care of patients takes money, money, and more money. Quality care can be bought at a price. . . ." Of course, good care does not come cheap, but is money alone enough? Patients who pay high prices for medical care may, and often do, receive far poorer care than indigents treated in dingy wards of city or county hospitals. Imposing architecture, carpeted corridors, and a TV set in every room are not accurate barometers of the quality of medical care rendered in a hospital. But if the Federal Government really means to reshape "the health-care system so that high quality medical care is available to all at a price they can afford," indeed Congress will have to come up with "money, money, and more money."

The simple fact is that no real improvement in the quality and availability of medical care can be expected until we come to grips with the critical problem of the shortage of doctors. Here in America, the cornucopia of the world, I see patients with acute appendicitis or other surgical emergencies lie around hour after hour until complications finally develop—all because of a shortage of medical personnel. A country that depends heavily upon the importation of foreign graduates, often poorly trained, to shore up its sagging manpower structure can look forward only to a further relative decline in quality. There is enough blame for the scarcity of physicians to pass freely around. The *Journal of the American Medical Association* said editorially in late 1969 that the organization recognized "ten or more years ago that the supply of physicians would not be adequate and [was] exerting strong pressure for increase in the number of schools and in the size of existing schools." This was a barefaced misstatement of fact. The AMA bears a heavy share of responsibility for the medical manpower shortage, and unfortunately despite much brave talk, Federal Government efforts to increase the number of doctors have been equally shortsighted.

Paralleling the distressing shortage is an equally serious maldistribution of physicians, who are less than enthusiastic about practicing in the urban and rural slums, where the need for their services is great indeed. The problem is not a new one. Almost a century ago, John Shaw Billings had this to say:

> A young and energetic man who has spent six years in obtaining a University education, and four more in the study of medicine as it should be studied, will not settle in certain districts, in part because he will have acquired tastes which will make his life unpleasant in such places.

Appalachia is such a "certain district"; the urban slum is another area where doctors find "life unpleasant." Nor is it merely a question that they could make more money elsewhere. Doctors want to practice medicine in places where they can have the stimulation of constant contact

with competent colleagues, where they have facilities to
do their work well, and have available specialists to handle
problems beyond their own competence. They want to
send their children to good schools, and their wives want
a pleasant social life. No doctor likes the idea of walking
down a dark city street infested with dope addicts who
know very well that there are narcotics in that little black
bag. Would you? Doctors are human beings too. How then
are we going to provide the inhabitants of the "unpleasant
places" with medical care?

Perhaps the place to start is with a definition of the
health that we are seeking. Two hundred years ago, Dr.
John Morgan, founder of the University of Pennsylvania
Medical School, defined health as "that choice seasoning
which gives a relish to all our enjoyments." Anthropologist
Ashley Montagu also expresses it poetically: "Health is
the ability to love and sickness is the inability to love." But
the more technical definition of the World Health Organization better suits our purpose: "Health is a state of complete physical, mental and social well-being, and not
merely the absence of disease or infirmity." The emphasis
is on a *total* adjustment to one's environment. I do not
agree, therefore, that poverty is a pathogen—a cause of
disease—or that poverty is associated with a high incidence of disease. *Poverty itself is a disease.* The poor are
certainly not in a "state of complete social well-being" and,
therefore, by definition are not in good health.

In fact poverty is the most common American disease.
It afflicts twice as many people as does the second one, ailments of the heart and circulatory system. From the
slums of New York to the migrant worker farms of California, there are pockets where millions are born in the

stench of poverty, live in it and die in it, leaving only a legacy of poverty to their children. For as every social worker knows, poverty begets poverty. Poverty is an hereditary and chronic disease: in New York, Philadelphia, and some other metropolitan areas, there are children who are the fourth generation of their families to have been on welfare.

The time-honored responsibility of the physician has been to prevent and cure disease and to alleviate suffering. Can the physician prevent poverty, cure poverty, or alleviate much of the suffering caused by poverty? What is there in a physician's background and training that would enable him to grapple with this most common of diseases?

The poor everywhere have large numbers of children whom they cannot feed properly. The doctor may be able to treat some of the symptoms of malnutrition, but he certainly cannot provide the food that would have prevented the trouble in the first place. Poor children in the South run barefoot because their parents cannot afford shoes. Bare feet pick up the parasites of hookworm. Giving those children shoes would do far more to eradicate hookworm than all the efforts of the medical profession. Almost 50 percent of the babies delivered at many municipal hospitals are the children of "walk-ins"—women who have never seen a doctor until they arrive at the emergency room in labor. If everything is not perfectly normal, can the obstetrician at that twelfth hour undo the results of nine months of neglect? Violence in the urban slum is reflected in a high homicide rate. The emergency room surgeon can only remove the bullet or stitch up the knife slash; sympathize though he does, he alone cannot change the social and human conditions that led to the crime.

Some suggest that an answer may be found by enlisting the cooperation of the poor in planning and operating the health system, but the concept of community involvement raises some interesting questions. Who speaks for the consumer? At elections to choose their representatives, the turnout is invariably small. Studies have shown that health care ranks low on the poor man's list of priorities: if he feels passable today, he is less worried about the possibility of needing a doctor next week than he is about how to pay the rent that is due tomorrow.

Moreover the poor are usually uneducated and lack both the background for reasoned decision and the patience to effect results. Consequently, many well-meaning poor become discouraged by the fact that they cannot work immediate miracles, and they soon stop participating. Some of those who remain have bigger mouths than intellects. For example, at public meetings militants have been known to arise and scream, "Fuck technology! Fuck technology!" "Maximum feasible participation" of the poor is not without its hazards; in health as in most areas, amateurs can rarely match the record of professionals.

Of course, physicians too may act amateurishly when they stray outside their own fields. At an almost totally unproductive 1969 White House conference on Food, Nutrition and Health (which cost the taxpayers roughly $1 million), a Georgetown University professor of pediatrics proposed a new right for the poor: "I know that many will use food stamps to buy Cokes and potato chips or trade them to buy liquor, but the poor should have the same right as anybody else to spend money foolishly." Of course they should—when it is their money. But taxpayers' money? Your money and mine?

A better solution, of course, would be to provide them with the opportunity to earn more money of their own. The health record of the poor is closely tied to the "culture of poverty." As Dr. Egeberg put it, "You can't prescribe medicine to be taken at 8 A.M., noon, 4 P.M. and again at 8 P.M. for people who don't even have a clock in the house." Question: Do we restructure health services to answer that problem—e.g., send a nurse around four times a day to give the patient his pill—or do we furnish him with a clock?

I have raised some thorny questions in this chapter, and they are not new ones. Rather they arise from complex, long-established social patterns, and here is the rub. There are no quick, technical solutions to social problems; ending poverty and racial discrimination will be far more difficult than transplanting a heart or putting a man on the moon. To move a poorly informed and apathetic public against the opposition of those with vested interests in the status quo cannot be easy. But solutions are not made easier by those who insist that the only answer is to destroy everything we have, the good along with the bad. And assertions that the doctor-patient relationship in private practice is "frequently one of mutual resentment" or that medical practice is "one of the last of the pushcart industries" cannot be allowed to go unchallenged.

I have no pat answers for all our vexing socioeconomic dilemmas, but this is no license for me to evade the issues. I do not intend to duck them. I approach these questions as one who has had long, hard, practical experience in dealing with the problems of individual patients. No matter how many miraculous new devices may come along, no matter how many brilliant new techniques may be discovered, no matter how many helpful assistants the doctor may be able to use, every case comes down to one essential: an individual doctor trying to help one person with a particular problem. In the last analysis, the patient and the doctor are face to face and alone together.

I think an approach from the standpoint of a working doctor is badly needed. The opinions of the nonphysician experts and of the nonpracticing physicians have been abundantly ventilated. Those in the front line of health service are rarely heard from. Lay experts, stressing "greater efficiency" and "more productivity," frequently equate doctors with production-line workers, patients with machines, and hospitals with factories. At the same time, they tell doctors not to adopt the dehumanizing, bulldozing attitudes of industry and admonish us never to forget that the patient needs generous doses of TLC (tender, loving care).

We hardly need these admonitions. Most of us are well aware that a man's nervous system is not the same as the wiring of a machine. Nor does anyone have to spell out to practicing doctors the consequences of our mistakes. We know that if it bungles some part of a Chevrolet, General Motors can send out recall letters to the buyers and have the fault repaired. Doctors cannot correct an ineptly performed operation as easily as a faulty brake mechanism can be replaced.

The economic problem is less the cost of good health care than it is whether we are getting our money's worth in quality. Assessing quality requires judgments based on the *science* of medicine, about which economists know little (even though merely having been patients qualifies them as experts on the *art* of medicine). But there are some points on which doctors and economists can agree, such as the necessity of budgeting in advance the costs of the actual medical care.

Washington's decision makers have frequently made the pilgrimage to the ivory towers to enlist the help of the academicians. But care in a medical school environment is something that relatively few patients ever experience, and it is quite different from the care provided on Main Street, USA. The patient with a rare problem, who receives highly complex care in a major medical center, is properly appreciative of it, but he would nevertheless view with considerable alarm the thought that automation and "health teams" will replace the personal visit to a doctor in whom he has confidence.

I am no expert on all phases of health care, and I make no claim to offering comprehensive coverage of medical socioeconomics. I discuss areas with which I am familiar largely on the basis of personal experience. Hence I may be charged with over simplification. So be it. I am not persuaded that complexity in itself has any virtue.

My intent is to be constructive. I have no desire to blow the whistle on medical institutions. The professional abuses I shall cite are intended to educate, not titillate, the public, but I make no apologies for exposing in blunt terms what I consider serious deficiencies of medical care in this country. A health-service system does not exist to benefit doctors, nurses, or hospital administrators; it exists to benefit patients.

If my therapeutic approach sometimes appears radical, I can only plead my surgical background. Sometimes a deeper incision hurts more at first, but allows the patient to recover more quickly in the long run. At least I hope that no one will be able to summarize this book the way a critic capsulized a White House press conference: "Well, Nixon declared that the medical system is dangerously ill, and then he prescribed two aspirins and a Band-Aid."

2

THE MAKING OF A DOCTOR

LIKE presidents and movie stars, doctors are made, not born (although moments after I had arrived in this world, my mother looked at my hands and announced firmly, "He's going to be a surgeon!"). But how differently they are made! The doctor's formula for success is study, study, and more study. Unlike starlets and would-be presidents, the medical student needs no PR man or makeup artist. The aspiring beauty in Hollywood may need some artificial padding in front, but the medical student needs plenty of natural padding behind to sustain him through the long nights of poring over his books. As Sir William Osler insisted, "The master word in medicine is work; the stupid man it will make bright, the bright brilliant and the brilliant student steady." Medicine is obviously not the place for those who would solve the problems of the world by chanting "Hare Krishna" all day long.

The prospective physician must become at home in a whole new world—the human body, its anatomy and its physiology, normal and abnormal. He must learn the precise language of that world as he becomes familiar with a bewildering array of diagnostic and therapeutic tools. An astronaut learns the complexities of an Apollo spaceship in a comparatively few years, but the machine has yet to be built that is as complicated as the human organism.

To learn how to handle this intricate and delicate mechanism, a physician usually spends four years in college, four years in medical school, and one year of hospital internship, which is really a working apprenticeship under the constant eyes of senior men. At this point he usually receives his state license to practice and may, if he chooses, go out and hang up his shingle. In the vast majority of cases, however, he elects to stay on in the hospital as a resident, taking training in some specialty for from three to five more years. Then he may take the examination offered by the specialty board in the field he has chosen, and, upon passing, be duly certified as a specialist. He is now deemed by his colleagues well qualified to practice medicine—to "cure sometimes, relieve often and comfort always."

Is he really well prepared to assume those awesome responsibilities? If the pervasive clamor for change in medical education is any criterion, he is not. According to their critics, medical schools are largely staffed by research-oriented faculties, and they turn out clinicians who, peering through the long, narrow tunnels of their specialties, can see at the other end only a disease, not a person, much less a family or a community.

Dr. Leonard D. Fenninger, former director of the Bureau of Health Manpower, makes a typical analysis: "Existing arrangements for the preparation of people in the field of health and for the delivery of health services are inadequate to meet the expectations of the public." People in the health field "are not cognizant of social need" because medical students are not trained "to think about the cultural, economic, social and political factors that influence the health and lives of men." There are many variations on this theme, but altogether the symphony sings of the need to indoctrinate medical students more fully in the behavioral and social sciences.

For some, not only the problems of American society but the problems of the entire world rest on the shoulders of that contemporary Atlas, the physician. Harvard surgeon Dr. Oliver Cope defines medicine's role in global terms: "Our society is in trouble. It is bewildered. There are great social inequities. After two world wars in our lifetime, we have barely enough sense to realize that we are teetering on the brink of the third. From a third, the world will not come out the same as we know it. *The world is sick and needs help. . . . Medicine perhaps can give the help, if we plan well*" (italics mine).

The medical campus rebels have redefined the role of the physician. As one of them, S. Alex Stalcup, president of the Associated Students at the University of California San Francisco Medical Center, put it, the doctor must now conform to "the broader experience and broader perspective of contemporary culture." Having personally decided upon the road the doctor should travel, he arrogantly added, "The entering student in medical school is probably a much finer physician than the aging clinical genius of ward-rounds fame." Cultural anthropologist Margaret Mead, who has joined the ranks of breast-beating oldsters who say that if they are young, they must be right, seems to agree: "Nowhere in the whole world are there any elders who know what the children know . . . There are no elders who know what those who have been reared in the past 20 years know about what the next 20 years will be." No wonder the militants are ready to take over! If the newly matriculated student is actually a better doctor than his professor, if by some miracle he can really read the future, then students and teachers should indeed change places.

There is no doubt that we can expect continued pressure for drastic revisions in the curriculum. The new doctor is supposed to be able to cope with such worldwide problems as nuclear war, overpopulation, and famine, as well as with the domestic agonies of festering slums, polluted air and water, choking traffic, avaricious corporations, monopolistic unions, alienated youth, racial conflict, and political corruption. I have no doubt that the solutions to these problems will do more for the world than a knowledge of the microscopic picture of intracapsular glomerulosclerosis in the kidney or an understanding of B-glucuronidase activity in cholestatic liver. But just what is the role of the doctor in modern society?

Despite all the faultfinding, American medical education and training is recognized the world around for its excellence. We now hold the position that Padua held in the sixteenth century as the center of medical learning in the world. Perhaps President Nixon's former science adviser, Lee Dubridge, had the answer to the paradox when he said, "Success has led only to rising expectations and to mounting accusations of failure." So we can expect continued carping at medical education by those who insist that doctors can cure all the ills of society.

The rise of our medical schools to their unassailable world preeminence did not just happen. Those who ignore the triumphs of medical education in this country suffer from historical amnesia. A century ago there was scarcely a medical school in the country worthy of the name. As many as 460 medical faculties were licensed to grant degrees, but they were mostly diploma mills with entrance requirements a sham and instruction almost nil. Most of these schools folded, but only because they were poor business ventures, not on their merits, or rather their lack of merits. Of the 160-plus schools in existence in 1900, fewer than half a dozen required college preparation, and only Johns Hopkins and Harvard provided outstanding medical education. The meccas for medical learning and research remained in western Europe, where such giants as Virchow, Ehrlich, Pasteur, and Koch impressed visiting Americans with the advanced teaching at their clinics.

A remarkable reversal took place shortly after the turn of the century. The AMA, founded in 1847 "to promote the science and art of medicine and the betterment of public health," had been weak and ineffectual in its early years, but it took a long step toward improving medical education by establishing a Council on Medical Education in 1904. The council formulated minimum standards and surveyed the existing medical schools, grading them A, B, and C—acceptable, doubtful, and hopeless. Each school was told its classification; the public was not. Despite this secrecy the unacceptable schools created such an uproar that the AMA found it expedient to table the entire matter. But not for long. The AMA recovered its nerve and sought the aid of the Carnegie Foundation for the Advancement of Teaching for an even more thorough study of the entire medical educational process. For a salary of $3,000 plus traveling expenses, the foundation engaged Abraham Flexner for the job. They got the medical bargain of the century.

Flexner was sharp-eyed, tough, persistent, and incorruptible. Of even greater importance, he was not a physician and so had no qualms about trampling on the sensitive toes of doctors. That proved to be the essential ingredient of success.

He personally visited 147 American and seven Canadian schools, and he was shocked by what he found. At the school in Salem, Oregon, he asked to see the physiology lab. "It's upstairs," the dean told him. "I'll bring it down to you." He returned bearing a single device for recording blood pressure. In Des Moines, Iowa, doors with such signs as "Anatomy" and "Physiology" were found to be locked, and the keys were conveniently unavailable. Instead of boarding a train that night, Flexner returned and gave the janitor a $5.00 bribe to open the rooms. The laboratories were devoid of equipment.

The Carnegie Foundation expected Flexner to lay his findings on the line: "The attitude of the Foundation is that all colleges and universities, whether supported by taxation or by private endowment, are in truth public service corporations, and that the public is entitled to know the facts concerning their administration and development." The AMA, in its *Journal* of August 14, 1909, endorsed that statement.

Dr. William H. Welsh of Johns Hopkins advised Flexner to make his report "a thorough exposition of observable or admitted facts, without glosses and without omissions." Flexner took the advice, and his report, published in 1910, hit with megaton force. "Blatantly advertised" commercial medical schools were labeled "disgraceful" and "shameful."

Chicago, with fifteen schools, was called "the plague spot of the country." The University of Buffalo's Medical Department was dismissed as "a fiction."

The cries of outrage were earsplitting. Flexner was called "unfair," "prejudiced," and worse. He was accused of misrepresentation and warned of lawsuits; even his life was threatened. The AMA, however, stood squarely behind him, and the editor of its *Journal* welcomed a lawsuit so that the "public [might] be acquainted with the facts."

The vituperation evoked by the Flexner report was matched by its impact. Almost half the country's medical schools had to close down within ten years; more went into eclipse later. Moreover, the schools that remained open were forced to upgrade medical education to a substantial degree. Flexner forced the beginning of a process that has continued ever since.

At the same time, two parallel movements contributed to the rising eminence of American medical education and training. One was the development of the full-time medical school faculty. Originally most teaching was done by men who made their livings from practice and who gave a few hours a week to the medical school, usually as unpaid volunteers. In 1913 Johns Hopkins, aided by a $1.5 million grant from the Rockefeller Foundation, established the first strictly full-time faculty. Other schools soon began to follow this example, employing, if not the entire faculty, at least the clinical department chiefs and other top men on a full-time basis. The movement was a natural outgrowth of the rapid expansion of medical science with its resultant trend toward specialization. It led to marked improvement in the quality of both instruction and patient care. In addition faculty members who no longer had to maintain large practices were able to devote more time to research, with a consequent elevation of this important function of medical schools.

The movement toward full-time faculty and other improvements had the backing of the AMA, which was in its Golden Age in the years immediately preceding World War I. Its leadership was not a collection of medical politicians, but was drawn from the great names of medical education and science. Its well-circulated *Journal* was highly regarded and unsurpassed in influence. Conditions were ripe for continued progress in medical education, and another long step forward was taken by the establishment of the specialty boards with the strong support of the AMA.

At that time there was not—and there still is not for that matter—anything in law to prevent anyone with a license to practice medicine from calling himself a specialist. Ignoramuses and outright quacks could and did call themselves specialists in anything they chose, and an uninformed public had no way to tell whether what glittered was indeed gold or merely pinchbeck. The real specialists were banding together in learned societies, such as the American College of Surgeons, but these existed primarily for the mutual exchange of the latest thought and scientific information and were of little direct help to the public.

It was clear that something needed to be done to improve the quality of specialist training and to protect the public from the incompetent. As a result the specialty societies and the AMA began to establish boards of examiners to test the qualifications of future candidates for specialty status. The first of these, the American Board of Ophthalmology, was organized in 1916 to certify those physicians who wished to limit practice to diseases of the eye.

At the same time, residency training programs for future specialists were established in the best hospitals. Standards for these programs were set and are maintained today by the AMA and the respective specialty boards. The young doctor may elect to take a hospital residency for several years, during which he will be under the direct eye and close supervision of qualified seniors, learning and working under their direction and being gradually allowed to do more and more as his experience and competence increase. Upon satisfactory completion of such a program, he may take his board examinations and be certified. The system works well—so well that a patient who is being looked after by a senior resident in a topnotch residency training program receives excellent medical care. Today 20 boards examine and certify doctors in 34 specialties, and their certificates may be relied on as evidence of professional competence, at least as of the date on which they were issued. It pays a patient to scan those dull-looking scrolls on the doctor's wall!

After World War II, the Association of American Medical Colleges—an old organization long regarded as a kind of sociable "Deans' Club"—began to take on a new life, a process that has accelerated in recent years. Its Commission on Medical Education, organized in 1925, became more active in encouraging innovation and experimentation in medical schools. The AAMC was instrumental in developing the Medical College Admission Test, which in 1947 began to apply a uniform standard of proficiency to candidates for entry to medical schools. It cooperated in the establishment in 1952 of the National Intern Matching Program, which made it vastly easier for hospitals and medical graduates to find one another.

This, in barest outline, is the half-century story of the metamorphosis of medical education in the United States. It is a saga of courage, determination, imagination, and progressive thinking that has produced several generations of the most highly skilled, superbly qualified medical professionals in human history. Certainly the system has its shortcomings and imperfections. Any human institution does, and this is especially bound to be true of one that must continually adapt to new breakthroughs in science and technology. Under such circumstances there are bound to be lags in some places and unsuccessful experiments in others. Even the noisiest of our campus rebels admit to the professional skills of our graduates and are mainly skeptical of their ability to solve the sociological, economic, cultural, and political problems of our society.

Many medical students are leading the charge to sweep away the "irrelevancies" of the curriculum. Dr. Robert Glaser, former dean of Stanford's Medical School, commented: "Our students are indeed leading the demand for a new order of things. . . . At no time in my professional career have I found the students to be so critical of their educational experience and so displeased by it. . . . They are also distinctly more concerned with society and its problems."

Note this:

The young medical student of today has a good grasp of knowledge and a high level of social consciousness. The first year medical student is familiar with the social phenomena of the day—from urbanization, industry, world problems, land and food to the specifically medical areas of insurance and hospitalization. In comparison with the medical student of 20 years ago, the student of today has a much higher degree of social awareness.

These words by the Magnuson Commission were *written twenty years ago*, in 1951. The people to whom Magnuson gave such high marks for their "high level of social consciousness" are the very same ones who are now being denounced as "businessmen" and "biological technicians."

This is not a new refrain:

> The amenities of professional intercourse and the obligations of medical men toward each other and the public were perhaps better observed [in the past]. . . . Then the doctor . . . was the trusted friend and counselor of every family to whom he ministered. He shared their joys, soothed their sorrows. . . . Now the doctor is regarded more in the light of a tradesman or a mechanic. . . . The strong ties of gratitude and affection have ceased to exist. Relationship is now placed upon a more commercial basis, and for this the profession is more to blame than the public.

That speech was delivered to the Illinois State Medical Society—in 1882.

Are doctors merely money grubbers? Are most of them vapid Philistines who are unconcerned about the social problems of the world? I know of no statistics purporting to show that doctors are either more or less concerned about our social ills than history teachers, architects, or bus drivers. Should we be?

It boils down to the scope and responsibilities of medicine and how to prepare physicians to fill them. No one questions that our primary responsibility is to heal the sick, and everyone agrees that our medical schools are not producing enough doctors to do that job adequately. But is it also our responsibility, as physicians, to "create a peaceful, prosperous and just society by working to improve the physical, emotional, social and economic well-being of our fellow men," as was claimed by a medical student leader addressing the 1969 AMA Congress on Medical Education?

I think not! The doctor's education and training already takes longer than that of any other profession. How can he cram into it enough extra knowledge to enable him to tackle the host of complex and difficult issues bedeviling our society? What medical subjects shall we leave out to make room for all the new courses? I must point out that while other people may be better prepared to deal with social problems, no one else can do the doctor's job. Somebody has to mind the medical store. Somebody has to stick around the hospital, if only to repair the cracked heads of the more violent social reformers.

Let there be no misunderstanding: I am in no way advocating that medical men shirk their social responsibilities. No one is more aware than the physician of the environmental and socioeconomic problems that plague his patients. Many doctors are, and all should be, socially aware human beings and citizens. Along with nonphysicians, doctors attend school board meetings, write letters to the editor, march for civil rights, and join political parties and activist movements, each according to his individual light. I salute Dr. Benjamin Spock's battle against the war in Vietnam, not because he is an eminent pediatrician, but because he risked jail for his personal convictions rather than remain silent in the face of an outrage to his conscience. I admire Dr. Christiaan Barnard's outspoken criticism of South African apartheid, not because of his pioneer work in human heart transplantation, but because his personal convictions were so strong that he refused to back down before savage attacks and personal threats.

And so I am in complete agreement with the students who say that doctors should be concerned about poverty, racism, and the environment. Shouldn't bank presidents also? Television newscasters? Plumbers? Indeed, shouldn't everyone be concerned? Concern for the underprivileged is one thing; the ability to do something about it is another. Slum housing is bad for tenants but profitable for landlords. Making it unprofitable is clearly beyond the physician's capabilities as physician.

It should not be forgotten either that a sizable proportion of the medical profession does devote itself exclusively to community problems. Many doctors have never set a fracture or delivered a baby, but concern themselves instead with community medicine, public health, and prevention. They run birth control clinics, track down cases of venereal disease, inoculate whole populations of the poor against numerous ailments, and devote themselves to discovering and eradicating the causes of ill health. There is nothing new about this. The public health doctor stands in the honored tradition of the medical profession. Both the doctor who handles the health problem of the community and the doctor who treats individual patients play a vital role in elevating health standards.

The medical educator and writer, Dr. Howard Rusk, stamped today's medical students as "a different breed" who are willing "to practice in the ghettos or on desolate Indian reservations." Some medical students are already sure of their superior social outlook and proclaim that their generation is "not as much interested in financial success as was perhaps the medical student of 20 or 30 years ago." I wonder. There have always been some doctors who care little for monetary reward. There are dedicated men in the US Public Health Service today who travel long distances through the Alaskan wilderness to visit remote Eskimo villages. There are earnest young general practitioners signing up for service in slum clinics. I salute them all.

I have also seen many young men who settled down to general practice in some small town throw in the towel after two or three years and come back to the hospital to take a residency. They did this not just for money; many of them had been doing very well. They did it because of the narrowness of the life, the lack of intellectual stimulation, the restricted social activity, and the poor quality of the schools. How many of today's crop of graduates will opt for the Navajo Indian reservation, rather than Santa Barbara, for Harlem, rather than Westchester County? How many will actually *stay* there? Based on my experience, the number will be precious few.

Indeed, some of the medical activists are already learning the lessons that only a bloody nose can give. For several summers the Student Health Organization obtained Federal grants for various summer projects designed to aid the disadvantaged. To their surprise they often found themselves rejected as interfering outsiders. Even when that was not the case, they discovered when summer had ended that no basic improvements had been made. Students reported the "agonies" of "disillusionment," "disappointment," and "frustration." One of the founders of SHO, Dr. William Bronston, came to the conclusion that the projects had been "romantic sensitivity trips, which really did not change anything fundamentally." He was right. The students may have felt good "doing their thing," but they actually accomplished little.

The militant activists are everywhere a small minority. Their fellows may enjoy the rumpuses the radical leftists kick up, but they do not always take the noise seriously. Witness the following tongue-in-cheek manifesto, which appeared in a campus publication at the University of Southern California:

The cadres [students and janitors—but not faculty] set forth the following ten (10) nonnegotiable demands, which must be met immediately if the hospital is not to be bombed or burned down:

1. The Dean must make an immediate public confession of guilt for the barbaric policies which the School of Medicine, as an instrument of the establishment, has hithertofore pursued.
2. Since they are most in tune with enlightened and useful social ideas, cadres alone shall be permitted to determine admission to the School of Medicine.
3. Each cadre shall grade his own examinations and shall be the sole judge of the adequacy of his work.
4. No material shall be taught which is not of immediate clinical relevance. Such relevance shall be determined by second-year cadres.
5. Nothing shall be taught which is not fully in accord with the teachings of Herbert Marcuse, Chairman Mao Tse-tung, and other philosophers of the Revolution. This applies particularly to the warnings of some such men regarding the dangers of science and technology.
6. No less than 1/10 of curricular time shall be devoted

to sessions for thought evaluation and self-criticism, so that useful social opinions may be furthered, and counter-revolutionary ones corrected.

7. No research shall be permitted which is supported by the United States Government, or which might conceivably be used in any manner to cause dehumanizing technological progress or to hurt people adversely [i.e., to hurt them in a nonrevolutionary manner].

8. To insure that they develop the proper social attitudes, all faculty must perform custodial work, the amount of which shall be determined for each professor by the cadres.

9. The cadres shall decide on the continuance of all faculty on a year to year basis.

10. The cadres shall be given sufficient time to radicalize the nurses.

Obviously not all medical students look upon Dr. Che Guevara as their hero!

I believe that year in and year out, medical students are medical students; only the problems change. There were just as many involved and aware students when I went to medical school in the late Depression years as there are today. The current crop may talk louder and get nationwide television coverage, but the major difference I see in this age of affluence is that today's young graduate drives a bigger car and starts to play the stock market earlier.

I deplore the exhortation that we add such subjects as urban planning and cultural anthropology to the medical school curriculum. Walter Lippmann called this kind of thinking "globalism" when it is done by our State Department. He warned, and rightly, that in attempting to police the entire world, the United States overextended itself with consequences that are now all too apparent.

Medical globalism would be equally wrong for the same reason. In a similar vein, Dr. Sherman Mellinkoff, dean of UCLA Medical School, pointed out,

> The question is not whether the world is more imperiled by overpopulation or by one child's meningitis. The question is which set of problems a particular individual is preparing himself to cope with. Political scientists, physicians, plumbers, fiscal analysts and agronomists are all needed, and as individual citizens they should be concerned with national and world affairs. But if a physician is not well educated as a physician, he will not, *ipso facto*, become a great sociologist.

Doctors are only part of the health team. When confronted with problems that are beyond their competence, medical students should learn to refer patients to social workers, family guidance counselors, clinical psychologists, visiting nurses, and other allied professionals. (They should also learn that reducing the rat population is a job for exterminators, not physicians.) But as concerned individuals, students need not, and should not, neglect the vexing social issues of the day. Nor, despite what a few students may think, do most of their teachers want them to. Most of us agree with what Abraham Flexner said half a century ago, that the best doctor "is first of all an educated man."

Curricular reform is no simple task. For one thing, there is a strong thrust to shorten the period of medical education and training, which up until now has been growing ever longer. This movement was stimulated by a study of medical education made some years ago for the AMA by a commission headed by Chancellor John S. Millis of the then Western Reserve University, now Case Western Re-

serve. He observed that doctors were both starting practice ever later and retiring ever earlier. Afterward Mr.
Millis plotted the curves of the two trends and found that
they would cross shortly before the year 2000. By that time
doctors will retire on the day they begin practice!

To avoid that paradoxical situation, the Millis Commission proposed that training be shortened and suggested as
one method abolishing the internship year and permitting
students to go directly from school into residency. That is
already permitted for nine specialties, and others seem
sure to follow. But because the specialty boards rightly
insist that the educational advantages of the internship
year not be lost, many of the essentials of that year must
now be covered in medical school.

Many schools are seeking to place more emphasis on
philosophy, ethics, and other humanities. (The medical
school of the State University of Pennsylvania at Hershey
has a theologian as a full-time faculty member.) Almost
every school has been giving its students more elective
time to pursue their own special interests. Most are intro-
ducing their students to the bedside earlier and giving
them more clinical training. All this without sacrificing the
essentials of the basic scientific curriculum!

This has been no easy undertaking, especially in the
older medical schools, where long-established patterns
have to be drastically altered. Powerful department heads
are naturally reluctant to have their baronies disturbed;
teachers of traditional subjects do not want to see them
curtailed. Despite such problems, even the established
schools *have* been moving forward toward more progressive methods of teaching. In many of the new schools, de-
partures from the old curricula are quite radical.

As I have noted, also to be crammed into the four years of medical school are the ever-mounting new developments in science. "We know that half of the factual material we teach today will either be proven false or superseded in five or ten years," says Dean Mervin Duval of the University of Arizona. "So we are trying to teach, not facts, but how to solve problems." Medical school today is but the beginning of a lifelong process of education, and faculties are puzzling over not only what to teach, but how to teach.

Finally there is one fundamental problem in every school: how to adapt to the rushing tides of this world without losing the principal value that we have now—the ability to turn out highly qualified doctors. A system that has been turning out the world's best physicians must not be destroyed, only improved. It is not surprising that thoughtful men tamper with this system only tentatively and after much deliberation.

Let me emphasize that the current nationwide surge of curriculum revision has been rolling for a long time *without* the prodding of medical students. The movement began as far back as 1952, when a thoroughgoing revision was put into effect at Western Reserve, and it has been fermenting in other faculties ever since, long before the current wave of agitation started. It may be that the recent campus rumbles have lent new urgency to faculty deliberations, but at best they have only served to accelerate changes that were already well under way.

I firmly believe that the professionals, the medical educators, must continue to have the final voice in the content of the curriculum. Certainly we should listen to the students; they may be saying something new. We should accommodate their wants as far as we can without jeopardizing their education, just as we let them choose their own work projects. But students have no built-in crystal balls; the young man today can hardly tell what knowledge he will need as the physician of tomorrow. Faculty members may not have crystal balls, either, but they do have experience, and that is still worth a great deal.

Some students argue that they want to become, let us say, dermatologists, and therefore ask why they should bother to learn about the anatomy of the foot or the blood supply of the stomach. They would do away with the core curriculum and learn only what they regard as relevant to their future specialties. This would lead to more of the very narrowness and disease orientation of which today's students complain. Whatever his specialty, a doctor is treating a whole person, not merely one part of the body or one set of symptoms. A dermatologist who does not realize that his patient's skin lesions may have an internal cause and a psychiatrist who tries to relieve a man's disturbances by analysis when he should be suspecting a brain tumor—neither of these physicians is a whole doctor.

Moreover medical specialties are subject to sudden and dazzling change. Years ago a principal part of the practice of the ear, nose, and throat man was removing mastoid bones in cases of ear infection. With the coming of antibiotics, that common operation overnight became a rarity, and ENT men were a dime a dozen. As a natural consequence, the number of young doctors entering that field dropped sharply. Recently many new operations requiring a high degree of skill have been developed, and now we do not have nearly enough ENT men to perform them.

What antibiotics did to the ENT specialist of some years

ago, another scientific advance could well do to some other specialty tomorrow. If a member of that specialty then wanted to broaden his field and take up some other line of work, it would be back to Square One in medical school for him if he had also skipped the core curriculum. The change would be far less painful for the man with a well-rounded education.

Medical students have about the same qualifications to make judgments about medical education as the sick have to prescribe for themselves. It is easy to use catch phrases like, "Medical education is too important to be left to medical educators" or students should be taught "to think less and feel more." But the fact is that medical educators have certain technical abilities that enable them to treat the sick; the students do not have these abilities. One has a perfect right to decide whether his new house is to be English, Spanish, or contemporary in style, and then decide whether his children will each have a private bathroom or share a common one. But only a fool would try to dictate to his architect such technical details as the strength of the roof rafters or the depth of the foundation. It is certainly not clear to me how noneducators can be expected to outperform educators in the field of education. Nor is it clear why an emotional doctor who "feels" is better than a cool-headed one who "thinks." There is nothing, of course, to keep a thinking doctor from also being a compassionate one.

At some schools, pressure has gained students a full voice on the curriculum committee. In my view, however, medical schools are not meant to be democratic institutions and cannot be run by simply counting noses; the educational content must not depend upon a consensus of the students. To give them that power is to substitute the untried desires of the many for the demonstrated excellent performance of the few. The students may want to spend more time on the cultural mores of slum dwellers or on marriage counseling. The faculty may believe that this time may be more profitably spent in learning to differentiate acute appendicitis from gallstone colic, diabetes from an overly active thyroid, or a heart attack from a perforated peptic ulcer. What comes next? A vote?

Medical students are not imprisoned; they are not barred from following their own bents to a very great degree. If one wants to spend his summer working in a slum health center, he may do so with the blessing of his dean. His expanded elective time gives him a wider opportunity to pursue his own interests than his predecessors ever had.

Students should be less concerned about the lack of opportunity that some claim exists within the medical school than about the fact that too many potentially good doctors never get to medical school at all. Right now our medical schools are turning away one fully qualified applicant for every one they accept. It is certain that even that unhappy figure does not tell the full story. No one knows the number—though it is surely substantial—of bright young men and women who would become excellent physicians, but who never even apply for admission because they are discouraged by the amount of time and money needed for a medical education.

Only about 10 percent of medical students come from the economically lower 50 percent of the population. Can we not completely subsidize a young college graduate when nothing but money is preventing him from becoming a badly needed physician? Tuition and fees account for less than 5 percent of the more than $1 billion we spend annually on medical education. Obviously no great hardship to the Treasury would result if the Government picked up that last 5 percent and added a little for the students' living costs. Our total investment in medical education has risen from $10,000 per student in 1926 to more than $100,000 today. Much of this increase reflects the vastly increased amount of research being carried out at medical schools, research financed almost entirely through Federal grants. There is no need here to enumerate the health benefits we have all gained from this research; we agree that this is money well spent. Is it not just as important to produce the doctors we need to apply that research and to insure that qualified young people have the opportunities they deserve?

As things stand now, many of the more affluent students go abroad for medical education. In 1970 there were 615 US citizens studying medicine at the University of Guadalajara in Mexico and more than 700 at the University of Bologna in Italy. Of all the licensed physicians now practicing in Rhode Island, a greater number are graduates of Bologna than of any other single medical school! To my mind it is a national disgrace that American young people must go abroad to seek opportunities they are denied at home. Even the option of studying abroad is denied to the poor, and this is of special significance for minority groups. The black minority makes up 11 percent of our general population but only 2.2 percent of our physician population. This disproportion bids fair to continue for a long time, since fewer than 3 percent of present medical students are black. In dentistry the outlook is even more bleak, since the proportion of black dentists is actually falling, from 4 percent in 1940 to 2 percent in 1965.

The small number of blacks in medical schools is not the fault of the schools. While many of them once may have discriminated against Negroes, as some of them did against Jews, under today's social pressures the discrimination, if it exists at all (at least outside the deep South), is in reverse. Medical schools are going out and actively recruiting qualified black students the way college football coaches go after star high school quarterbacks. One Southern dean who thought he had nailed down a brilliant black medical school prospect was a little resentful when the young man announced that he had had a more attractive offer from Harvard. The dean felt a certain grim but understandable satisfaction a little later when the same student dumped Harvard for a still better deal from the University of California!

The schools are finding the recruitment of qualified young blacks extremely difficult. For one thing, the economics work against medicine as a career. The black who has graduated near the top of the class at a good college has the world for an oyster. Even though a medical school offers him full tuition and expenses, it will still be eight, nine, or ten years before he begins to earn a living. He can choose any other profession and start earning far sooner. And meanwhile there are plenty of corporations ready to offer him $12,000 or $15,000 right now. If the graduate is the son of a poor tenant farmer or if his mother has been scrubbing floors in white ladies' apartments to get him through college, as is often the case, he can hardly be blamed for being tempted by money that will help his family immediately.

Secondly, because they have suffered from discrimination all through their schooling, many black students who want to study medicine simply are not as well grounded as more fortunate white students. This is not peculiarly a problem of the medical schools; the trouble starts before the child even enters primary school. The problem is one for society as a whole. The medical schools are doing what they can; one, Albert Einstein, offers disadvantaged students a year of postcollege study to help them catch up before they enter the medical school. Others are relaxing their admission standards in favor of disadvantaged students and offering them special help after entrance. The deans universally and stoutly insist that they will not lower graduation standards; the fellow who starts out behind must catch up to and equal his fellows by the time he gets his MD degree. It is to be hoped that the deans mean it; it would be a cruel hoax on the individuals and catastrophic for society to turn out doctors who offered patients substandard treatment.

All in all I am not alarmed about the controversies swirling about our medical schools. I would be more concerned if there were not pressure for breaks with the past. I am not interested in preserving the status quo, but I see no crisis, no need for tearing our schools apart. Our schools *are* changing with the times. Curricula have provided students with the intellectual tools for becoming superb doctors, and I am not aware that the schools have resisted social change.

Unfortunately not all our entering students are educated men, in the full sense of that word, before they come to the medical school, and some have difficulty adjusting to the philosophy, morality, and ethics of Hippocratic medical practice. Some of them must be nurtured along and gradually imbued with the ideals and discipline of the father of medicine from the isle of Cos. I confess to indignation when I hear of medical students going through the wards of municipal hospitals wearing turtleneck sweaters and dangling peace medallions in the faces of sick old ladies. Some patients have refused to be examined by the more hippie types because they did not believe that they were doctors.

The students are right in demanding that we do not waste their time with irrelevancies, but, in the interest of their future patients, neither should we be overly permissive. Tender plants can wither and die if they are overwatered.

3

WHERE ARE THE DOCTORS?

IN recent years a new type billboard has sprung up along some American highways. These signs do not direct you to the Shady Rest Motel, invite you to feast at Joe's Eats, or tell you how to increase your sex appeal by smoking Brand X cigarettes. Instead they say, "This Town Needs a Doctor."

Where are the doctors? At least 5000 communities have none at all, though they want them badly. Some towns have put on fund-raising drives to build and equip up-to-the-minute medical offices, offered without charge to any doctor who will come in and use them. A quarter of a century ago there were a dozen doctors practicing in or near Dyersville, Iowa. In 1970 there were three, of whom two were in their mid-sixties and near retirement. One of these two was an osteopath, and the other was cutting back severely on his practice because he had had a heart attack. In the hope of attracting more doctors, the 18,000 residents of Dyersville and vicinity raised the money themselves and in 1969 opened a gleaming new 90-bed hospital. To staff it the town wrote to dozens of medical societies and to every U.S. hospital with an intern training program. No luck. A year after Dyersville Community Hospital opened, 70 of its beds were empty because the only doctor on its staff could handle no more than 20 patients at a time there. He had not had a day off in months.

Dyersville is unusual only in that it built a hospital. In Illinois alone in 1970, the medical society's placement service had a list of 150 towns desperately in need of doctors. Among them was one town of 22,000 persons with only one doctor and a six-town trade area with none at all. Indeed, more than 500,000 Americans live in rural counties without a single MD.

The small towns are not alone in their plight. Studies of the decaying central areas of many cities—including New York, Chicago, Los Angeles, and Baltimore—show that while they were well served medically in their better days, the doctors have followed their middle-class patients in moving away. In 1930 the East Garfield Park section of Chicago had 212 physicians. In 1970 there were just 13 doctors remaining there to serve 63,000 poor patients. (At the same time, a single building in a fashionable part of Chicago had 40 doctors, more than three times the total of East Garfield Park.) It is not that Chicago is poor in medical talent. Its Cook County has 183 doctors per 100,000 population, as compared to the national average of only 131. Similarly, New York City has 278 physicians per 100,000 population, but precious few of them are to be found in the slums. In the Watts section of Los Angeles, there is only one doctor for each 2900 patients. There is no reason to believe that conditions are much better in the slums of your city, wherever it is.

There is no longer the slightest doubt that our medical manpower shortage is genuinely acute. The problem has passed from serious to drastic, from alarming to critical, and now verges on the disastrous. No responsible authority any longer questions the need for more doctors; the only questions now are how many, by what means, and how fast we can provide them. In my opinion we need just about as many as there are qualified candidates for medical school—which is double the number we now enroll—and we need them as quickly as possible.

Medicine has been pulled in two opposing directions in recent years. On the one hand, newer technology, therapeutic progress, greater use of auxiliary personnel, and urbanization have greatly increased the doctor's productivity. The GP who used to make house calls all over the countryside by horse and buggy now can see three times as many patients who come to his office by car. When I was starting out in practice, a patient who had had a hernia operation remained in bed for three weeks with a pillow under his knees. Now the patient walks on the very first day, and he is out of the hospital in two or three days, leaving the bed free for the next case. I remember walking the wards of Cook County Hospital when perhaps 50 percent of the surgical cases were draining osteomyelitis, or draining empyemas of the chest. Now antibiotics have made such cases infrequent, and surgeons can devote their time to other matters.

On the other hand, the physician's increased productivity has been more than overbalanced by other factors. There has been an explosion of demand for medical services because we are better educated to the need for them than our parents were, we are better off financially, and we are far more likely to have health insurance. The aging of a population brings with it more cases of chronic disease. At the same time, complex new diagnostic and therapeutic procedures make heavy demands upon the doctor's time. Open-heart surgery, for example, was unknown twenty years ago, but now takes hours and hours in the operating room for a whole team of doctors, not to mention the large amount of time that must be spent in the preoperative workup and in postoperative care.

Moreover, today a greater percentage of doctors are going into teaching, research, administration, and public health. These are all desirable medical functions, but their attractiveness to increased numbers of physicians leaves a smaller percentage of the profession available to care for individual patients.

The doctor shortage was discussed in 1968 in an editorial in the *Los Angeles Times*: "The United States is suffering from a malady that could have an increasingly serious effect upon the health of the nation—a scarcity of doctors." The editorial concluded: "Congress and the state legislatures can pass laws and vote money, but the prognosis for American medical care basically depends upon the response of the American Medical Association."

The AMA's recent response to this challenge has been to call for an "immediate and unprecedented" expansion of medical schools. One recent AMA president, Dr. James Z. Appel, called for doubling the doctor output as soon as possible.

It was not always so. The AMA should be less than proud of its former shortsighted and irresponsible official positions. In the mid-1930s, money was scarce and doctors' waiting rooms were empty, so Dr. Walter Bierring, AMA president, advised medical schools to cut down on the number of graduates. The AMA was more interested in practicing physician birth control than in bringing health care to the millions who could not afford to seek it.

By 1949 thoughtful authorities were alarmed over the tightening medical manpower shortage. Alabama's Senator Lister Hill, an astute and forward-looking champion of better health care, introduced a bill to provide a ten-year program of Federal matching funds to help the building of new schools, to support the operation of existing schools, and to give thousands of scholarships to needy students. The senator was two decades ahead of his time; his bill passed the Senate, but was killed in the House of Representatives largely because of the AMA's intense lobbying against it. When proponents of the measure predicted a severe doctor shortage by 1960, the AMA smugly countered, "It certainly seems more reasonable to expect a surplus than a deficit of physicians in 1960."

In 1951 President Truman's Magnuson Commission accurately prophesied a shortage of 45,000 doctors by 1960. The AMA's response was vitriolic. That estimate was scorned as "statistical propaganda" and an illustration of the "intellectual poverty of the Commission."

Official medicine in 1952 stressed productivity and relied almost exclusively upon the "rising output per physician" to prevent a shortage. Five years later the then president of the AMA could say, "We continue to hear alarmists spread the false idea that there is, or will be, a doctor shortage in America. Personally, I see no crisis or emergency in the present or future supply of physicians."

In 1959 a group of consultants appointed by the surgeon general, the Bane Commission, again warned of the shortage, calling for a 50 percent increase in the number of medical graduates by 1975. Although the commission far underestimated today's needs, the AMA continued its frivolous blindness to the medical deficit. Even as late as 1965, officials were still pooh-poohing the shortage and perhaps reached the height of irresponsibility to the public with this arrant nonsense, uttered by Dr. John C. Nunemaker, then assistant secretary of the AMA's Council on Medical Education: "There's a tremendous demand for more doctors, just as there is for luxurious cars and yachts. But we can't show there's an actual shortage, especially as compared with the rest of the world." Which part of the rest of the world could the AMA have had in mind? Ethiopia? Tibet?

In mid-1966 the organization called an abrupt about face. Only a few months after it had circulated a "Physician Population Fact Sheet," which disparaged those who had a gloomy outlook on the doctor supply, the AMA suddenly became "well aware of the *drastic shortage* of health manpower" (italics mine).

Since the AMA's switch to a "short" position, some of its leaders have courageously admitted the organization's previous mistakes. Executive Vice President Dr. Ernest B. Howard said the "AMA was late to recognize" the problem, while Dr. Milford O. Rouse, president in 1967–68, called the old policies mistaken, albeit "well-intended," and asked the profession to face its "most important single challenge—the distressing shortage of physicians."

More recently the AMA joined the Association of American Medical Colleges in urging medical schools to do no less than to "accept as a goal the expansion of their collective enrollments to a level that permits all qualified applicants to be admitted." Since that means at least a doubling of present enrollment, this enlightened position by two such prestigious organizations should surely have provided the final impetus for a meaningful augmentation in the doctor output. As the astronauts say, all systems should have been "Go."

But no! In a remarkable reversal, the Johnson Administration, squeezed by economics and overinvolved in the Vietnam War, markedly cooled its attitude toward turning out more doctors. The shift understandably dismayed those who had looked for clear sailing once the obstructing fog of official AMA policy had lifted.

The change in emphasis was manifested late in 1965 at a White House Health Conference, where the participants displayed far more interest in the utilization of doctors than in their numbers. Shortly thereafter, as the AMA was convulsing with the realization that its old policy was leading to disaster, a smaller but equally important conference met at Fort Lauderdale, Florida, to discuss "The Crisis in Medical Services and Medical Education." The medical elite of Washington and their academic advisers were there in force. The participants were persuaded of the need for reforms that would match those instigated by Flexner in magnitude, but a clarion call for a dramatic increase in the number of medical school graduates was strangely missing. The conference report took due note of the thousands of unfilled positions in approved residency training programs and the thousands of positions that were filled by foreign medical graduates, but then recommended an increase of *only 4 percent per year* in the number of MDs. Such a spit in the ocean would hardly dent existing shortages, much less meet the increasing "needs of a growing and changing nation"! The conference stressed the reorganization of medical education and service, recommending the training of "primary physicians," prepaid group practice, changes in medical school curricula, and the development of "medical assistants in various categories" (later to be called "physicians' assistants").

It soon became obvious that the Fort Lauderdale conference's attitude was shared by the Department of HEW. In February 1967, HEW conducted a study on the "reasons behind the rapid rise in the price of medical care." The report recognized the intense pressure generated by the rapid rise in demand for health services and the relatively slow growth in the number of doctors; it did not stress balancing the rising demand by equally increasing the supply of physicians. Surely a recognition that the law of supply and demand has not yet been repealed would have been of major help in moderating costs.

The report made seven recommendations, including encouragement of group practice and development of the physician's assistant. It also emphasized the need for greater use of medical skills so as to increase productivity and played a theme that has been frequently repeated in Washington: if each doctor in the country increased his productivity by 4 percent, that would add up to more new medical care per year than is provided by the annual output of our medical schools. Washington had come round to the increased productivity position which the AMA had just thrown out. Dr. Philip R. Lee, then assistant secretary of HEW, observed that "when a choice must be made between spending on medical education to produce more doctors and on research and development (of health-care delivery systems), the choice should be research and development." (However, a few years later, he changed his tune and bemoaned the lack of educational opportunities for qualified students: "What a tragic waste of human potential when the country cries for more physicians.") In support of Dr. Lee's choice, think tanks were enlisted to apply to health care the methods they had used to develop new weapons systems, and the halls of HEW resounded to the exciting lexicon of these medical engineers.

Federal support for expanding medical education had never been much more than a token. Now funds to help build new schools were cut from an approved $203 million in 1967 to a request of $84.8 million for the budget of 1968.

The sentiment of the Johnson Administration was perhaps most cogently summarized by the report of the 1967 National Advisory Commission on Health Manpower. This blue-ribbon group, appointed by the President, took a "new look" at the need for more doctors. It recommended a "substantial expansion of existing schools and continued development of new schools." (What is "substantial?" 4 percent? 50 percent? 100 percent?) But then it cautioned against a "crash effort to increase production." The commission settled into the comfortable position that "the setting of new goals should be tempered by the realization that medical school enrollments are already increasing at the fastest rate in decades," a curious statement indeed. In the decade of 1950–59, the number of medical graduates increased by 23; the increase for 1960–69 was only 13. The commission repeated the familiar Washington refrain: "The crisis . . . is not simply one of numbers. . . . Unless we improve the system. . . ."

The fact is that regardless of how the system may be changed, the crisis is far and away most importantly one of numbers. The Department of Labor has estimated that the health-service demands for the decade 1966–75 require 6000 more medical school graduates per year. That is a huge increase over the 1970 output of 8000 graduates. It would require the equivalent of 70 new schools, and even that would be far short of our real needs. We would need an additional 20 schools to eliminate our dependence upon the 2000 foreign-trained physicians whom we license every year. The suggestion that we import even more foreign graduates as a temporary measure is fatuous. Cannot the world's wealthiest country supply its own medical personnel?

Moreover, it seems unlikely that we shall be able to count on even our present supply of foreign-trained doctors much longer. Most come from the underdeveloped countries of Latin America and Asia, countries that are no longer willing to subsidize the doctor shortage of the rich United States. Acutely aware of their own needs and of the cost to them of educating doctors, they are taking steps to stop the brain drain. In Haiti, the dictator, Dr. Francois "Papa Doc" Duvalier, has ordered that medical graduates no longer receive their diplomas, which are kept under lock and key at the medical school, so that if a doctor escapes he will have no professional credentials and be unable to obtain a license abroad. India now requires that physicians going abroad put up a substantial cash deposit, a kind of bail, to insure their return. Turkey and Iran have taken their own steps to halt this foreign aid in reverse. As they should! It is immoral—it is the height of cynicism —for us to import the doctors these countries so desperately need while at the same time we pump money into them to "stimulate socioeconomic growth." Yet if it dries up, this source of medical manpower will have a catastrophic effect on many of our hospitals, especially in the

East and Midwest, many of whose house staffs are predominantly foreign. Perhaps we need such a crisis to arouse the American public to the fact that we are not producing enough doctors of our own! What would it do to the hospitals of New Jersey, where 87 percent of all interns and 78 percent of all residents are foreign-born!

Who are the foreign doctors who come here? Some are among our greatest medical scientists, and their number includes several Nobel Prize winners. Others are little less brilliant. They represent the cream of the local crop who have come here for advanced training of a quality they cannot get anywhere else in the world. Usually they intend to take their new skills back home, but often they change their minds. They have learned to enjoy our unparalleled facilities. They have learned to do difficult and sophisticated procedures, while back home they know patients will die because they cannot perform those procedures without equipment and assistance that just is not there. To avoid frustrations they stay in the United States.

Such doctors are the rare ones. Others who come from the underdeveloped countries have usually had inadequate education and poor training. To them the language barrier alone is formidable indeed. Perhaps for most immigrants it is enough to have sufficient English to ask one's way about the streets of a strange city and order a meal in a restaurant. That is far from enough for a doctor. He must be able to communicate with his colleagues with scientific precision, using technical language of great complexity. He must also be able fully to communicate with his patients, and the possibilities for misunderstanding are immense. When the hospital ship *Hope* was in Peru, a volunteer American physician who spoke no Spanish was making rounds on his first day. Looking up from a bedside chart, he addressed a woman patient as "Senora Orina," throwing the entire ward into convulsions. A line on the chart that he had taken to be her name was actually an instruction to "save urine specimen." It may be only a comic incident to address a lady as "Mrs. Urine" when there are plenty of translators about, but there can be fatal consequences if an emergency patient cannot explain his injuries to an uncomprehending physician. Some hospitals have had to draw up glossaries of common American terms and slang for their foreign house staffs so that the doctor will know the difference between a sharp pain and a dull ache and so that when the patient says, "Gee, Doc. I feel lousy," the physician will not necessarily start examining his scalp in search of *pediculus capitis*.

Even beyond the language barrier, many of these doctors do not have the requirements to take the stiff test of the National Board of Medical Examiners; their education has not been up to American standards. Without constant sharpening, such skills as they have may deteriorate rapidly. John Lavin, associate editor of *Medical Economics*, paints this picture:

> In a small, underdeveloped nation right now, a young man is attending lectures at an ill-equipped, poorly staffed medical school that would be considered totally inadequate by U.S. medical school standards. In time, he will receive a diploma without ever having seen a patient. Then he will take a multiple-choice examination based on National Board tests—but with the tougher questions left out and the language simplified in consideration of his halting English. If he fails, he will take it again. And again. Passage will gain him admission to the United

States—but not to one of the better internships or residencies. They'll already be filled through the National Intern Matching Program. His background and language problem will lead him to a poorly supervised hospital with no medical school affiliation where the need for a house staff is great, the training poor. He will plunge directly into vital patient-care work, but his continuing lack of adequate training will severely restrict his development of clinical skills. For one reason or another—marriage or illness or some special hardship—he will be able to have his status changed from exchange visitor to permanent resident. After one year of internship, he will take a state board examination in a state that hasn't failed a candidate in 10 years. He will pass and take his place in the mainstream of American medicine.

Mr. Lavin does not exaggerate. In 1966, 60 graduates of one medical school in the Philippines took the Illinois state licensing examinations, and 49 of them—80 percent—failed. When 25 graduates of the same school took the state examinations in adjoining Indiana, every one passed! Is there any doubt that an ill-equipped foreign graduate can set up practice in the United States?

Some 2000 foreign graduates achieve permanent physician status in the United States every year, about 20 percent of the total number licensed annually. There are now 40,000 licensed foreign doctors—15 percent of the active physicians in this country—and the revised Immigration and Naturalization Act of 1968 encourages still more to come from underdeveloped countries.

It is not surprising that the high hopes of President Johnson's International Health Message of 1966 died at birth. The brave rhetoric that promised to "build clinics and provide doctors" to the underprivileged world simply could not be fulfilled. We have sent pitifully few doctors to the backward areas of Asia, Africa, and South America. We have been taking doctors from those areas. Let there be no mistake about it—we are a doctor-debtor nation.

Not so the Soviet Union. They do have doctors to export. More than 500,000 physicians (three-quarters of whom are women, incidentally) and 460,000 *feldshers* (subphysicians) and midwives provide patient care in the Soviet Union, far more manpower than is available for the same purpose in the United States. Though the Soviet population is only 17 percent larger than ours, their medical schools turn out 350 percent more graduates. This vast training program makes it possible for the Soviets to build and staff hospitals in North Vietnam, Nepal, Burma, Algeria, Ghana, Yemen, and other underdeveloped countries. The number of doctors that the Soviet Union exports annually to emergent countries is reported to be about 2000. It would take the output of 25 average sized American medical schools to match that number.

Those who are familiar with the tremendous impact that has been made in foreign lands by a single American private effort, the hospital ship *Hope*, can appreciate the effect that this much greater Soviet foreign medical aid is having, not only in improving the health of backward people, but in establishing a humanitarian image for the Soviet Union. Some may argue that Soviet medicine is inferior to ours, but that is an irrelevant quibble. Her physicians look good indeed compared to the witch doctors of Africa and the herb dispensers of Asia.

Aside from what we should be doing abroad, we have a crisis in health manpower at home, here and now. The doctor shortage is not felt only in slums and small towns. More than a thousand medical school faculty posts are unfilled.

So are many thousands of hospital house staff positions. There is no way of knowing for sure how many patients in state mental institutions who might be restored to useful life are instead left to rot in custodial care because there are no psychiatrists to treat them. We need tens of thousands more public health physicians, roentgenologists, anesthesiologists, and pediatricians. Our general practitioners are seriously overworked, many so badly that they cannot find time to keep up with rapidly changing medical technology.

The shortage of house staff bears with particular damage upon our public hospitals, which are largely held together by their interns, residents, and hope. I have in my own experience repeatedly seen patients in need of an emergency operation arrive at a hospital and then wait for surgery because someone else is in even more critical condition; there simply were not enough staff available to open a second operating room. I know of one hospital that has posted a sign in its emergency room explaining to the public that patients are not cared for on a first-come, first-served basis because the critically ill must take precedence. It is obvious that this is the only way in which the hospital can work, but it is equally obvious that the number two patient cannot always get the best quality care.

It seems clear that the Public Health Service estimate putting our doctor shortage at more than 50,000 is hardly inflated. Even if our health-service machine were perfect, which is far from the case, it obviously cannot function without sufficient operating manpower. Unless the shortage is relieved, our level of medical care can only deteriorate.

The only effective answer to a scarcity of a commodity or service, if one cannot lessen the demand, is to increase the supply. In this case demand is certain to increase markedly as more and more of our newly aroused disadvantaged people seek better medical care than they are now getting. It will take a medical school expansion program of Gargantuan proportions to overcome present shortages, to meet that increased demand, to fulfill our moral responsibility to the "have not" countries of the world, and to counterbalance the decreased supply of foreign doctors which we may expect as the underdeveloped countries move to plug their brain drains.

No one will quarrel with platitudinous exhortations to use our existing manpower more productively, and I am all for any efficiencies that will not sacrifice the quality of care. But the consideration of most pressing importance is the number of doctors. I suggested to the profession back in 1966 in the pages of *Medical Economics* that the medical school output must be *doubled* as quickly as possible, and since then many others have come to agree. Nothing should stand in our way at this point.

We are blessed with plenty of qualified candidates for admission. Today's college graduate is superior by every objective standard to the graduate of a generation ago. He has frequently learned as much science in high school as his father was taught in college, and this advancement continues at every stage of premedical and medical education. Students who take the Medical College Admission Test are averaging higher grades than ever before, and the rise is chiefly due to better performance by applicants who are later refused admission. Medical educators generally agree that these young people are qualified; the problem is that the schools, as presently set up and financed, simply do not have room for them.

Of this I am certain: even if scholastic barriers to admission had to be lowered slightly (which I do not concede to be the case), future graduates will be capable of rendering far better care than at least 50 percent of the MDs, osteopaths, chiropractors, faith healers, and cultists now attending to the ills of the American people. There is so much new knowledge that today's graduate is bound to be a better doctor than the average graduate of some years ago, even if he is not as innately bright.

Nor is there any doubt that we have the technical and financial ability to undertake the expansion that I envisage. Poland has doubled the number of its medical schools in the past twenty years. West Germany has less than one-third of our population, but admits more than 50 percent as many medical students each year as we do. Can we not do as well as two countries that lay in smoking devastation as recently as 1945? We have the people, the tools, and the money. All we need is the will.

Only the crashiest of crash programs will do the job as rapidly as it needs to be done. We are used to that. Characteristically we remain apathetic about important and controversial problems until the pressure of events forces us into explosive—sometimes hysterical—action. But then the job usually gets done.

We did it in medical education during World War II. Under the fierce pressure of those days, medical schools worked twelve months a year rather than nine. They turned out doctors in three years instead of four, and interns served nine months instead of twelve. The doctors who were turned out under that program were, and are, good physicians. A recent study of their present performance showed that they are the equals of the four-year men who were graduated immediately before and after them.

Our present approach is two-pronged—to build new schools and to expand existing ones. We need the new schools badly. For one reason there are important parts of the country that do not have enough schools to accommodate local young people, and there are other important areas with no medical school at all. The location of new schools should be planned to fill these gaps. Such planning can be of major help in relieving the maldistribution of doctors. The Montana boy who goes east to medical school faces strong temptations to stay there. If first-rate education and training were available at home, he would be far more likely to marry a Montana girl and to form other strong personal and professional ties that would keep him there. Studies have shown that doctors usually begin to practice in the areas where they have taken their residencies. New medical schools are also needed because they are not encrusted with the hoary traditions, fixed customs, and established faculty baronies that characterize some of the existing schools. Indeed, many of the most innovative ideas in medical education are coming to fruition in our new schools.

For our present needs new schools have two major disadvantages: they are very expensive, and they take a very long time starting up. No school started today could hope to get off the ground for much less than $100 million, and even that amount is highly conservative. The new Penn State school, which took its first students in 1968 at Hershey, began with a gift of $50 million from the Milton S. Hershey Foundation. It is already receiving state support. Costs at Mount Sinai in New York are approaching $100 million. Because of the staggering cost, it is likely that we will never again see the founding of another private medical school. The money must come from Government.

There is also a very long lead time between the decision to start a new school and the graduation of the first class. The Hershey school broke all records in that respect with an eight-year span, and that was possible only because it had money in hand, plus an unusually able and energetic dean. Ten or twelve years is much more common, and longer times are not unusual. A new medical school for the University of Massachusetts has been in the planning stage for twenty years and has yet to get off the drawing boards. To this time must be added another one to five years for postgraduate training before the new doctors are ready to begin practice. Badly needed though they are, we cannot count on new schools to be of much immediate help in relieving our present problem.

That leaves us with just one alternative: to graduate more doctors from our existing schools. This will cost us money. It will require some dislocations and discomforts. It will raise cries of outrage from some conservative and comfortable faculty members, but it must be done.

I propose that, on the average, existing schools (except for those that have recently launched a substantial expansion program) increase the size of their freshman classes by 15 percent annually for six consecutive years. Together with new school construction, this program would double the output of doctors in ten years.

Yes, this solution will create problems. Classes may have to be larger than they should be. Professors may have to take some time from their research in order to give more time to teaching. There may have to be crowding and unorthodox hours. But however an individual school may work out the details, whatever minor sacrifices may have to be made, the medical profession would be reminded that it must never again lag behind a dynamic society. Medicine has defied the law of supply and demand and must now pay the penalty for that defiance.

Under this program a typical medical school now admitting 100 freshmen a year would admit 190 in the sixth year and would graduate 170 doctors a year at the end of nine years, allowing for about 10 percent attrition. Can it be done? Sweden is correcting her medical manpower problem by stepping up her medical school output so that the 1965 physician population of 8500 will reach 20,000 in 1980—a 135 percent increase in 15 years. Denmark is planning to increase the size of her graduating classes by 70 percent between 1969 and 1972. France started 21 new medical faculties in a single year, 1969. It *can* be done in the United States.

That is not to say that it *will* be done. The medical schools by themselves cannot possibly do it. Medical schools are tremendous financial liabilities. Tuition fees, now at all-time highs and still rising, cover only a token amount of the cost of a student's education. To make up the difference, private schools must depend upon gifts and endowment income, state schools on legislative appropriations, and all of them on Federal grants. For many schools in recent years, this support simply has not been enough. Many are extremely hard-pressed financially, and a few have even threatened to close their doors.

A new dimension of financial difficulty has lately been added for some schools by the rising demand that they provide new medical services to their communities. The teaching hospitals of private schools located in decaying central cities can no longer select only the patients they want for educational purposes. Instead they are now called upon to meet the medical needs of the whole poor population that has grown up around them. Many schools have responded magnificently to this new challenge, but at terrifying cost. Medicaid and local welfare usually pay but a fraction of the expense of caring for the poor who cannot pay for themselves, and so the medical school's hospital has become the locus of a financial hemorrhage, spurting the institution's green lifeblood out an open artery. To cite but one example, Temple University in Philadelphia lost $800,000 in 1969 on its medical center.

Even if the present needs of the medical schools are met, substantial support for expansion must come from the Federal Government. Present Federal plans fall far short of what is needed.

What is realistically required is a subsidy to the medical schools large enough to cover fully the costs of expansion, a subsidy to the student large enough to cover all the personal expenses that are beyond his own resources, and enough money to build the additional new schools that we require. A Senate subcommittee chaired by Abraham Ribicoff of Connecticut—who, it will be remembered, is a former secretary of HEW—proposed in the late spring of 1970 to double our present supply of doctors to 600,000 by 1985; he estimated the cost during the intervening period at $1.2 billion a year. That is considerably less than the $30 billion or so that it cost us to put a man on the moon, and to my mind would be money far better spent. Our annual health bill now exceeds $70 billion. Surely it makes good economic sense to spend 2 percent of that amount to train the doctors we need in order to get our money's worth. Will our leaders have the imagination to accept this thorny challenge, plus the skill and daring that will be needed to navigate an adequate medical education program through the rough waters of an economy-minded Congress?

I am acquainted with enough medical educators to know that many of them will resist an expansion program of this magnitude. Naturally enough they fear a dilution of the quality of medical education, whether it be due to the lower intellectual attainments of entering students or to exacerbation of faculty shortages. These dissenters must face the stark alternative. Tens of millions of Americans receive little or no medical care or are ministered to by practitioners far inferior to those who would be turned out by an expanded program. These people simply will not continue to accept so inferior a status. Either we devise means to give everyone adequate health services as a fundamental right, or involuntary methods will be devised for us. That would not be medicine's finest hour.

4

VANISHING AMERICAN: THE
GENERAL PRACTITIONER

AMERICANS remember the old-time general practitioner out of a Norman Rockwell painting: driving far out to a lonely farmhouse in the middle of the night to deliver a baby, wiping the brow of a feverish child, or draining pus from the chest by lamplight on the kitchen table. (In how many movies did we see the doctor take off his coat, roll up his sleeves with determination, and say, "Get me hot water—lots of hot water!" I never have figured out what he did with all that hot water.) The doctor was family counselor and friend, ministering angel, and miracle worker, all rolled into one.

I can understand and appreciate the sentimentality that surrounded him, the old-time GP. In actual fact he was, far more often than not, a little-sung hero. He did offer sympathy and kindness if only because, all too frequently, that was all he could offer. His little black bag held just about all the existing medical armamentarium, and that was pitifully small by today's standards. His drugs were not much better than those of which Oliver Wendell Holmes said, "If the whole *materia medica*, as now used, could be sunk to the bottom of the sea, it would be all the better for mankind, and all the worse for the fishes." The old-time doctor was forced to practice empirically rather than scientifically; most of the specific remedies that are commonplace today did not exist. His unhurried manner is readily understandable because he saw an average of only 50 patients a week, while today's general practitioner sees 200 or 250. Considering the medical knowledge and the tools available to him, he did, by and large, a magnificent job. As Sir William Osler said of the GPs of half a century ago, "They form the very sinews of the profession—generous-hearted men, with well-balanced, cool heads, not scientific always, but learned in the wisdom, not of the laboratories, but of the sickroom." Unquestionably the GP was the mainstay of our health-care system and largely responsible for the high esteem in which individual physicians have always been held. He well deserves to be remembered and honored for having rendered invaluable service.

But how does the GP fit in with the health needs of the future? Today he is slowly dying out, even though his well-meaning friends refuse to let him go in peace. Fewer and fewer medical school graduates are willing to enter general practice. The direction of training and practice has shifted heavily toward specialization, not only in the United States, but all over the world. As recently as 1931, GPs outnumbered specialists five to one; now this ratio is almost completely reversed. Physicians in general practice comprise less than 20 percent of the total physician population, and 18 percent of them are over 65 years of age. On the other hand, the number of certified specialists rose from 14,000 in 1939 to 112,000 in 1970, and there are many more specialists who have not yet been certified.

This is all to the good. For more than half a century it has been obvious that medical knowledge was growing too fast for any one man to encompass it all. Specialties and subspecialties have not proliferated merely because some doctors wanted them to do so; rather the proliferation of knowledge forced specialization upon the doctor who wanted to become proficient in one field. To become a top-notch doctor, he simply could not continue to treat "the skin and its contents."

One man can build a log cabin, and in a bygone era that was the way many homes were built. But today's modern home? What one man can pour the foundation, lay the brick, install the plumbing, put in the wiring, engineer the heating and air conditioning, connect the sewage lines, and hook up the telephones? The log cabin was much simpler, but we shall never go back to it. Given the complexities of today's life, specialization is inevitable in almost every field. Physicians would be far more vulnerable to criticism if they lagged behind lawyers, engineers, or construction workers, all of whom have become increasingly specialized.

Critics say that specialization has produced fragmentation of medical services and a shortage of doctors who are willing to provide "comprehensive and continuing care." Yet most people associate the best medical care with specialist care, and Americans increasingly want the best of everything. Sophisticated patients, from educated individuals to shrewd managers of union health plans, have long insisted on specialist care. Now middle- and low-income groups are demanding the same level of care, and rightly so. The all-specialist group practice clinic of which I am a member has provided comprehensive care for more than 80,000 families in the past twenty years. Our patients have not resisted—indeed they have welcomed—specialist care. At no time has the clinic had a demand for the services of general practitioners. Our internists are the family doctors for the adults, our pediatricians for the children. We serve a low- to middle-class socioeconomic area, and an appreciable percentage of our patients belong to minority groups. Our considerable experience certainly suggests that specialist care has now attained mainstream status in this country.

Yet there are those who seek to reverse this trend. They believe that if they can only give the dying GP a few whiffs of oxygen and a fancy cosmetic job he will spring up to life as good as new. Even the GP's best friends, however, admit that the old practice of giving him only a year's internship after medical school before he hangs out his shingle no longer prepares him to deliver high quality medical care. The idea is to keep the GP alive by making him too a specialist!

For many years the American Academy of General Practice fought for the establishment of a board to certify GPs as specialists. At last they won their battle, and in 1970 the first 2000 GPs took the examination of the new American Board of Family Practice. The 1700 who passed now sport on their office walls certificates proclaiming them to be specialists in family practice. These doctors and those who will pass future examinations are undoubtedly among the best qualified GPs, but are they *specialists?*

The AAGP and the ABFP are acting with the best of intentions and are setting high standards. For one thing, they are the first specialty which did not "grandfather in" anyone. When the other boards were established, some long-established practitioners were given certification without having to take the examinations; every FP must pass the examination. For another, every FP must prove he is keeping himself up to date by taking a new examination every six years in order to *retain* his certificate, something no other specialty requires.

The ABFP is novel in another respect as well. All other specialty boards are made up only of doctors in the appropriate specialty. The ABFP consists of ten GPs, plus one member each from the specialties of internal medicine, surgery, obstetrics-gynecology, pediatrics, and psychiatry. Cynics say the AMA politicans would permit establishment of the board only on the condition that these members be added to act as watchdogs so they could insure that the new FP would not encroach too far into their various fields. The general practitioners put a better face on the matter, saying that these members are there just to be helpful to the FP who must gain a smattering of knowledge in each of their fields.

Be that as it may, some of the members of the AMA's interspecialty council who voted for the establishment of the ABFP had serious doubts that they were giving birth to a viable baby. The political pressure upon them was immense; the AAGP has about 32,000 members, a very important chunk of the AMA membership. Some men voted to set up the board, despite serious reservations, largely because they did not want to be accused of killing something that so many of their colleagues wanted.

Under the new program, the training of GPs will be upgraded from the simple one-year internship to a three-year residency program. In order to provide comprehensive care, the new FP must learn something of each of the specialties represented on the ABFP, plus preventive medicine, epidemiology, and emergency medicine. He will be strongly oriented to provide care "within the context of the family and community" and will develop an "understanding of the interaction of cultural, social, psychological and environmental factors and disease." He will also be trained in "counseling and group dynamics, in order to properly treat the whole family and contribute to emotional stability." (Obviously only geniuses need apply.) Upon finishing this residency, the young doctor will be eligible to take the ABFP examination and attain his certification.

GPs believed that the establishment of certification, plus the acute doctor shortage, plus their own pressure, plus public nostalgia, however misguided, for the old-time physician, plus politics would lead to greater emphasis on medical education for family practice. They have certainly been proved right. No new medical school is complete without a department of family practice or community medicine, and such departments are springing up in the older schools like marijuana plants in a hippie's garden.

Politicians see family practice as the answer to their prayers. The Nebraska legislature mandated the establishment of a department of community medicine at the state university's medical school and gave the department its own special budget so that the money could not be spent for any other purpose. In 1969 the New York legislature, under prodding from Governor Nelson A. Rockefeller, decreed that all state medical schools establish "a department of general practice under the direction of a qualified general practitioner, courses of study under the supervision of qualified general practitioners . . . [and] a program of internships and general practice residencies in the hospital or hospitals affiliated with such respective schools." New Jersey's governor, William T. Cahill, declared in 1970 that medical school emphasis on research and the training of specialists had had "a catastrophic impact in our big cities" because there are not enough GPs. In a message to the legislature, he pointed out that 75 percent of medical school graduates now go into training for specialties which he said have little or no relevance to the immediate needs of city dwellers. He urged a law to consolidate control of New Jersey's two medical colleges under the state so that they could be made to "concentrate on delivering" GPs. The legislature passed the law. A bill has been passed by the Congress, with AMA support, granting medical schools $225 million in the next three years to help finance departments of family practice. Former senator Ralph Yarborough, sponsor of the measure, explained the philosophy behind it. "If you [medical schools] would go back to teaching family medicine as you used to do fifty years ago [sic], the Federal Government will assist you." That antiquated thought speaks for itself. President Nixon vetoed the measure, however, insisting that sufficient monies are being spent to push the growth of family practice.

At the same time, family practice residencies have been mushrooming. Though they were scarce indeed until recently, by the opening of the 1970–71 residency year on July 1, 1970, 46 such residency programs had been approved, one of them so newborn that it had not had time to recruit any residents. Such signs as these have the GPs jubilantly believing that they are on the way back to the top. Dr. Carroll L. Witten of Louisville, Kentucky, past president of the AAGP, happily predicted that "by 1974 50 percent of medical students will elect family practice as their specialty."

To my mind these optimistic predictions overshoot the mark by far. The fact that FP training is becoming so widely available does not necessarily mean that medical students and young doctors will elect that specialty. In 1970 there were just 286 young men and women enrolled in those 45 operating residency programs—most of them foreign graduates. At the same time there were nearly 40,000 residents taking training in other specialties.

I believe that the hopes of the GPs rest on several false assumptions. The first of these is that the American public can somehow be reeducated to prefer GP care over specialist care. If Governor Cahill is successful in his endeavors and if he is around years hence to pick the fruit of his labors when a horde of young GPs descend upon New Jersey's central cities, I wager he will find that more rotten eggs than bouquets will be thrown at him by angry citizens complaining that they do not want "second-class medical care."

Nor do I believe that the medical student ever again will elect to become a jack of all trades and master of none. The hard fact is that doctors *like* to practice as specialists, and there are excellent reasons why this is so. Realistically, no physician can acquire sufficient knowledge to become an expert in any phase of medical care if he spends his training time in a dozen different specialties instead of one. The proliferation of knowledge is just too great. The trend instead is in the opposite direction, toward the creation of new specialties and subspecialties. (Half a dozen are waiting in the wings for recognition right now.) The doctor who wants to excel has no choice but to concentrate all his energies in one field.

This leads to a second point. Status within the profession goes to those who *do* excel at a specialty. For this reason the GP has always been at the bottom of the pecking order. Whenever one of his patients becomes seriously ill, he loses that patient, at least temporarily, to someone who knows more about the problem than he does. Calling him a specialist in family practice will not change that situation one bit. It may give a glossy new coat of paint to the low man on the totem pole, but it will not move him a single notch nearer the top.

There is also a money problem: specialists generally earn more than GPs. Right now the manpower shortage makes this a relatively minor factor; GPs are doing very well, despite their much shorter postgraduate training. But adding two or three years to that training is likely to add little or nothing to their earning power, so there is no particular financial incentive to take the training. And if we ever come to the happy day when we have enough doctors to go around, the earnings gap between the GP and the specialist is likely to widen.

How then can we realistically expect the medical student to undertake a long postgraduate training program that will lead him only to questionable public acceptance, small promise of professional gratification or stature, and a dubious financial position compared to that of his specialist colleagues? Is he not far more likely to ask himself why he should set his sights so low when, with the same or little more training time, he can become a specialist? I would question the judgment of any student who did not at least ponder that question. Realists understand this. As Dr.

Robert Ebert, dean of Harvard Medical School, put it: "It has become abundantly clear in recent years that the general practitioner is disappearing from the American medical scene. Though the medical profession—tradition-bound and guild-oriented—has been slow to admit that changes in medical practice have taken place, medical students have not. They recognize the reality of the situation, and fewer and fewer wish to enter general practice." His statement is borne out by a poll of 1970 graduates of the Medical School of Washington University, St. Louis; of 71 new doctors, the number aiming for family practice was two.

Governor Rockefeller, Governor Cahill, and the other King Canutes cannot reverse this tide. They can and they are building troughs and filling them with water, but they do not have the power to make the medical student drink. More and more the role of the family doctor is being transferred to the internist for adults, the pediatrician for children, and sometimes when special long-term or recurring problems exist another specialist as well. Patients like this arrangement because the doctor can handle more of the serious problems than the GP can. Doctors like this type practice for professional reasons. The system is especially satisfying to both parties in the ever-increasing number of instances where the doctors work in medical office buildings or group practice clinics so that the patient need only walk down the hall if the services of another specialist are required. He finds comprehensive, continuous medical care under one roof. The fact that this excellent system of medical care is not yet available to all our people is no argument for reviving the general practitioner. Rather our aim should be to take advantage of the way both patients and doctors prefer medicine to be practiced and make a real effort to extend its benefits to those who do not yet enjoy them.

The GP can take solace in the fact that he is not suffering financially as he fades from the medical picture. When the supermarket forced the corner grocery store out of business, somebody often got badly hurt. Not so the GP. If after a few financially rewarding years he wants to specialize, he can always return to the hospital for further training, and his experience in general practice will stand him in good stead. If he decides to remain in general practice, with the shortage of doctors being what it is, he can count on prospering until he finally retires.

I have expressed my views about this vanishing American despite strong contentions to the contrary by organized medicine. AMA President-elect, Dr. Wesley W. Hall, has high hopes for the family practice specialist of the future. In a recent address to the Congress of County Medical Societies, Dr. Hall stated: "The family practice specialist is our best bet for organization of medical care for the benefit of the patient, for the optimum employment and application of scarce skills and facilities, and for the best use of the medical care dollar." I can only hope that this assessment of the family practice specialist, who has arrived "as if timed by Providence" according to Dr. Hall, is faulty crystal-ball gazing. If the new FP is indeed the "best bet" for curing the ills of medicine, medicine is dead. Absolutely dead.

5

THE DOCTOR CRIES FOR HELP

THE doctor is overworked and needs help. Who will provide it? Many people are talking about a new kind of health worker, a highly specialized "physician's assistant." This person will require far less training than a physician, but will relieve the busy doctor of many onerous tasks that do not require his full professional judgment. At a minimum the assistant will do such things as take the patient's case history, draw blood for laboratory tests, and perform some of those tests. He will explain to the patient matters that otherwise would consume the doctor's more valuable time. As Dr. Arnold I. Kisch, assistant professor of medical care organization at the UCLA, put it: "Communication-in-depth with patients regarding their medical and related needs could be handled just as well by a medical auxiliary. Such an auxiliary would receive the physician's diagnosis, prognostication and treatment plan, and would have the leisure necessary to communicate this information to the patient in a thorough and sympathetic manner."

Some assistants will have greater responsibilities. Pediatricians' assistants are being trained to give well-baby care, to prescribe some drugs, and even to make house calls in cases where the doctor has given specific instructions as to how the patient is to be treated. Nurse-midwives are being trained to deliver babies. Former medical corpsmen are being trained to undertake fairly complex duties.

Training programs of various levels of sophistication are under way in many places, and their number steadily increases. Some are quite sophisticated and have such prerequisites as a nurse's license or military medical corps experience. Studies may include anatomy, physiology, animal surgery, pharmacology, the uses and care of electronic instruments, and the history of medicine. It is too early to judge how the graduates of these programs will work out; pilot studies are under way and time will tell.

It is not too early, however, to look at the broad philosophy of alleviating the manpower shortage by using physicians' assistants. Actually, what is so new about the idea? What else but doctors' assistants are the hundreds of thousands of nurses, surgical and laboratory technicians, physiotherapists, occupational and inhalation therapists, audiologists, and the other health auxiliaries? It is ludicrous when people point to the use of dental hygienists by dentists to "increase productivity" and say doctors should emulate that example. We have been doing it for years. Early in this century, there was only one other health professional for every physician; today there are fifteen. It is not surprising that we use many more and more varied assistants than dentists do. After all, the mouth is a rather restricted area.

Yet I am skeptical about several aspects of HEW's enthusiasm for physicians' assistants, beginning with the nurse-midwife concept. I am well aware that the midwife system is widely used abroad and in some places works very well. In Sweden, for example, the vast majority of babies are delivered by trained midwives. A doctor sees *every* patient as often as may be necessary during her pregnancy, and if there seems to be any difficulty, he handles the delivery, too. But if a perfectly normal birth appears in the offing, the baby is delivered in the hospital by a midwife with the doctor standing by on call in case of unexpected complications. Due largely to excellent and universal prenatal care and to the fact that specialists handle all difficult cases, Sweden has a considerably better record than we have in mother and child mortality. Far too many of our people do not enjoy such advantages.

Sweden has a long tradition of midwifery, however; that is the way most babies have always been delivered there, and Swedish women find nothing unusual in the system. In most of the United States, that tradition died out with the passing of the frontier days. Most of our women would regard a return to it, and rightly, as retrogression. So would the women of some other countries; in Japan, for example, the midwife is rapidly being phased out of obstetrical care, and I simply cannot believe that the American woman, who will not even buy a dozen oranges at the supermarket unless they are wrapped in plastic, will turn back the clock. And, of course, she will adamantly refuse to change from hospital to home deliveries as has been suggested by a prominent health authority. Her hunger for luxuries will remain insatiable, and she will demand that the black-and-white TV set in her hospital room he traded for color rather than agree to a switch from hospital to home deliveries.

I do not think this view is negated by the fact that midwifery survives in deprived areas of Appalachia and the remote corners of Indian reservations. The practice is said to be well accepted by the poor who use New York's Bellevue Hospital, but that fact, if fact it be, is not persuasive either. That people who have little and know little must make the best of what is available does not mean that the many millions of more affluent Americans will accept the same treatment. The very poor of Appalachia and Harlem accept a diet of hog jowl and collard greens, too, but I have not noticed this dish on the tables of very many people who can afford beef.

Although the doctor shortage is worldwide, I know of no other industrialized country promoting a physicians' assistant program. Indeed Poland, which embarked on the training of *feldshers* as an emergency measure after the war, is now turning their training schools into medical schools. Perhaps physicians' assistants are just the thing for Ethiopia, where there is one doctor for every 95,000 persons, but if we have to accept them as working outside the hospitals or doctors' offices in this country, it would be only from economic necessity. Perhaps that is the only way we can man some posts in inner city slums or in remote, sparsely populated areas, but I hope not. That would mean two systems of health service with physicians serving most people and assistants serving the less fortunate, second-class citizens.

There are also other considerations. Where will we find the potential physicians' assistants without robbing Peter to pay Paul? We are already desperately short of people to fill existing jobs; our hospitals need 350,000 people of all skills who simply are not now available. Some large municipal hospitals have been able to fill no more than 30 percent of their budgeted nursing positions. A scattering of hospitals from Norfolk, Virginia, to Pasadena, California, has even been forced to shut down wards or floors because they could not find the people to staff them. Beyond current personnel shortages, an additional 750,000 people will be needed in hospitals by 1975 if we are to give optimum care. What is the net social gain if we take a desperately needed nurse away from the bedside to make her a pediatric assistant?

Another problem: former Surgeon General Dr. William Stewart acknowledged "an alarming dilution in the quality of nursing service" because the demand for nurses has increased so much faster than the supply. The shortage is directly attributable to the fact that we have dragged our feet about expanding nursing education, while concentrating on developing "assistant nurses"—practical nurses and nurses' aides. Will we learn from history or are we doomed to repeat it?

We would all like to increase physician productivity, but medical care is not an assembly line product. An essential part of it is a good relationship between doctor and patient. Can the doctor run his patients through an office assembly line, manned by others, giving the individual only the barest minimum of his precious time, and still preserve a meaningful relationship? The complaint is already widespread that many of us are too impersonal, too hurried. Yet there are those who foresee the day, as a doctor's letter to the editor of *Medical Opinion* put it, when "automation and teamwork take over and a new generation grows up relating to the machine, [and] the physician-patient relationship in all its present-day overtones will become a historical curiosity." "If that day comes," replies Dr. Roy Perkins, former director of AMA

Health Services, "I would not want to be a practicing physician. Still less would I want to become a patient."

I am sure that most practicing doctors, and most patients, agree with Dr. Perkins. Yes, physicians want more technical help, but they are understandably wary about placing yet another human barrier between themselves and their patients. Another and very important worry of doctors, if not of patients, is a potential increase in the danger of malpractice suits. The doctor is both morally and legally responsible for the actions of his subordinates. He is "the captain of the ship." If an assistant attempts something beyond his qualifications and if there is an unhappy result, the doctor could well find himself in court. Some anesthesiologists have had their malpractice insurance canceled because they used nurse assistants.

There is yet one more problem: the formal two- to four-year training of assistants in schools tends to force them into hardened molds. There are requirements for the course and by regulations for licensure which follow rigid patterns. A frequent result is that there are awkward corners where the assistant's training and the doctor's requirements do not jibe. Colorado, for example, has already set up a licensing law covering the new pediatric assistants who are being turned out in that state. That action is deplored by one of the country's most respected legal experts on medicine, William J. Curran, JD, of Harvard Medical School. Dr. Curran pointed out the wide variations among the many training programs now going on, the uncertainty of how the exact duties and responsibilities of assistants will work out; he argued that "such efforts (as licensing) merely solidify what should remain for some time a fluid situation."

An example of the harm that such freezing can do was given in *Medical World News* by Ray E. Brown, executive vice president of the Northwestern University Medical Center, speaking of hospital accreditation requirements. "The surveyor looks to see if the lab technicians are graduates of an approved school, forcing these jobs into the hands of the paramedical guilds and upping costs," Mr. Brown said. "The administrators say that with autoanalyzers, they don't need technicians. They can train a guy to do just that job. They say check his test results, not his diploma."

Just so. In our hospitals ward nurses are trained by the hospital and the medical staff for specialized work in coronary care and intensive care units, and they do it superbly. This pattern can serve as a model. Thousands of hospitals, group clinics, and doctors' offices can serve as training centers for health workers who will then be fitted to the jobs they do and the people they work for. These health workers can be turned out in one-quarter the time and at one-tenth the cost of training the kind of physician assistant that HEW is sold on. The programs can be tailored to local needs, state malpractice and licensing laws, patient acceptance, and the individual temperaments of both workers and physicians. This last is of no small importance: assistants must be accepted by doctors as well as by patients.

My own office assistant, a charming and intelligent woman, came to me with virtually no medical background. After a few months of training on the job, she was assisting me in minor operations; after a few more months she became my scrub nurse, for major operations in the hospital, and a very good one she is, too. In the office she performs such technical tasks as removing sutures and casts. I did not have to teach her to "unlearn" anything; from the beginning she did things my way. She does not hesitate to use medical judgment within her clearly defined boundaries. If a patient has injured himself and arrives with a painful and swollen ankle, she at once orders x-rays so that I can see the patient and the film at the same time. She learned both her skills and my needs on the job, the best of all possible places. A long, expensive training course, with classes in anatomy, physiology, and electronics would not have increased her value one bit. The kind of help she gives me is the kind most doctors need and want. Nor am I by any means the only one to have trained his own assistant in this way; many others have done the same. A person trained in the office is sure of patient acceptance; I never heard a single complaint from a patient as my assistant gradually took over procedures I had formerly done myself. The patient who is being wheeled into the cold sterility of the operating room is always cheered to see her familiar, smiling face and receive her warm greeting.

But let us go beyond my personal experience and look at the medical practice of a man who probably uses more physician assistants than any other doctor in the country. Dr. Paul Maddox of Campton, Kentucky, takes care of some 200 patients a day (and delivers 400 babies per year) with the help of a dozen assistants. These health-care workers were recruited from the community and trained in "about six months" to fit the needs of his rural Kentucky patients. When queried about physician assistants who had been exposed to two or four years of formal university training, Dr. Maddox dismissed the idea with a blunt, "they wouldn't be worth a damn to me." I'm with Dr. Maddox.

There is a real danger that in training physicians' assistants in long, didactic courses we may repeat a mistake made by the nursing profession. Seeking, quite properly, to upgrade their status, the American Nursing Association has vigorously promoted baccalaureate degree education and discouraged the hospital diploma programs. As a result the number of hospital programs has been decreasing, thus worsening the shortage. We need Indians as well as chiefs. I am all for training women for administrative positions and giving them every chance to earn them, but we need bedside nurses, too, and badly. Hence I am in favor of both types of training, not of phasing out one that has proved its usefulness over many years.

I am strongly in favor of training some categories of health worker on the job for the job they will be doing. An average high school graduate can learn to be a skilled operating room technician in six months, and he will then assume as much responsibility and contribute as much to society as anyone with skills of a comparable level. Some experts are concerned that such narrowly specialized, quickly trained technicians will have little "upward mobility." I am not much concerned about that. Many people choose jobs with little upward mobility: What promotions are available to truck drivers, bricklayers, or TV repairmen? Auxiliary health workers are predominantly female, the type of person who might like to be an airline stewardess! What upward mobility does a stewardess have? To many people good pay, good working conditions, and job satisfaction are more important. For those to whom upward mobility is important, there are other careers.

We have many thousands of empty jobs and we have many thousands of young people who could do and badly need those jobs. Why not bring them together in the simplest, shortest, and best way?

6

GROUP PRACTICE—A GOOD THING, BUT NO MIRACLE

I practice medicine as a member of a group. I am a devout believer in and a stout champion of group medical practice; if I were not, I should choose some other way to organize my professional life. I believe that group practice offers decided advantages to both doctor and patient that are attainable in no other way. Having made that much clear, I must add that I do *not* share Washington's touching faith that group practice is the cure for all our health-care ills.

Since the term "group practice" means so many things to so many people, let us begin by defining our terms. It is quite common for two or more physicians to share office space, equipment, and personnel as a simple, good business arrangement. As long as it is no more than that, they are still solo practitioners, not group practitioners. They may use the same x-ray machine, the same secretary may send out bills for each of them, and each may sign a monthly check for his share of the expenses, but they are not partners.

Partnership is another form of organization. The partners not only share expenses and facilities, but they also pool income and divide it according to some prearranged plan. They have a signed partnership agreement that is essentially no different from the agreements that would be signed by the owners of a dress factory or a stock broker- age firm. But doctors do not like the term "partnership" —it smacks of commercialism—so they often use the term "group."

Such an arrangement is sufficient to meet the HEW definition of group practice: "any group of three or more physicians (full- or part-time) formally organized to pro- vide medical services, with income from medical practice distributed according to some prearranged plan." The AMA's definition is substantially the same. Doctors orga- nized in this way enjoy some of the advantages of true group practice. (By covering for one another, they can enjoy uninterrupted time off for recreation and education; if Dr. A must unexpectedly take care of Dr. B's patient, the medical records are at hand.) But if the physicians are all of the same specialty, this is not really group practice, to my mind. For purposes of clarity in this discussion, I shall call this arrangement a "partnership."

To realize the full potential of group practice, the part- nership must be a multispecialty one. I would modify the HEW definition by saying, *to provide comprehensive care by at least five physicians, including the basic medical specialties.* There are four such specialties: internal medi- cine, pediatrics, surgery, and obstetrics-gynecology. A group including these specialists can provide a broad spectrum of care, and only the relatively rare problem would have to be referred out.

There is a further difference among groups in methods of compensation. Some groups are compensated by fees for service, as is my own. Others, like the Kaiser groups on the West Coast and like the Health Insurance Plan of Greater New York (HIP) on the East, derive all their income from prepayment. A few are mixed: the famous Palo Alto Medical Clinic receives about 85 percent of its income from fees for service and about 15 percent from prepayment.

Group practice, I think, provides a solution to the "dehumanization" of medical care. If Internist Dr. X is Mrs. Jones's family physician and she has to bring the baby to see Pediatrician Dr. Y or Junior to Surgeon Dr. Z, she still can get one-stop care under one roof. If Dr. X decides that she could see the obstetrician or needs an x-ray, it is only a step down the hall in either case. No matter how many different doctors the family sees or how many services are required, there is just one monthly itemized bill. It has been my experience that patients seem to feel just as much at home in the well-organized group clinic as they ever did with the old-time family doctor.

There are many advantages for the group doctor as well, beyond his ability to enjoy his free time uninterrupted. (Many of these advantages are available to doctors in medical partnership as well.) It is easier to provide efficient, high quality care when right at hand there is equipment and personnel that a single physician could not readily afford. A group can offer its members accident and sickness benefits, more reasonable insurance rates, and retirement plans that are unavailable to the solo practitioner. Does a patient have a puzzling problem? It is handy to have another specialist right down the hall. Many a patient has benefited from "corridor consultations" that he never knew occurred, much less got a bill for. Finally there are internal quality controls. Not only do group members have time for continuing education at medical meetings, but they also are continuously educating each other. They are well aware that even one bad apple could harm the good name of the whole group, and hence there is a constant pressure among the members to keep each other practicing at a high level. (I do not say this is true of all groups—there are good and bad groups, just as there are individuals—but it is certainly true of the better ones.)

The advantages of group practice do not accrue to the patient who goes to a member of a medical partnership composed of a single category of physician, whether they be all general practitioners or all members of the same specialty. The patient suffers all the disadvantages of solo practice: she must go to one place to see her internist, take her child elsewhere to a pediatrician, and go to yet a third office for an obstetrician. There is waste: the patient's records are duplicated in several offices. Care provided in this way is responsible for the complaint heard so frequently, "I don't have a personal doctor."

I do not intend by this to minimize the advantages to doctors of belonging to single-specialty partnerships or to belittle the quality of care provided either by those physicians or by solo practitioners; most of these men provide excellent care. What I am emphasizing is that they cannot provide *comprehensive* care, nor does the way they function alleviate the objections that some patients have to specialty practice.

The Federal Government is now actively encouraging the group practice of medicine. An office within HEW is devoted solely to that purpose. Under Title V of Public Law 89-754, the government offers to underwrite the construction and expansion of group clinics. The proposed Part C of Medicare would offer old people preventive services through groups. The government appears to share with others, and with me, the belief that this kind of practice is "the most satisfactory method of rendering private medical care to a community." Will all the king's men succeed in stimulating a mushroom growth in group practice? I hope so, but I am skeptical.

The growth of group practice received its greatest stimulus years ago when things were tough for doctors. (It may seem hard to believe now, but there were such times.) As a fresh MD, I wanted to intern at Cook County Hospital, where the training was superb. The intern's pay consisted of room and board, nothing more, not even cigarette money. (With uncanny foresight the hospital board recognized the evils of tobacco thirty years ago.) Activists at Cook County wanted to "see a little of the green" and petitioned the authorities for a salary of twelve dollars a month. The request was denied when the director argued that the hospital contributed so much to the intern's training that he should pay the hospital for the privilege of working there. I was also unhappy, as I remember it, about the fact that a patient in the 30-bed wards could not get a bedpan unless he tipped the orderly a dime. (I wonder what it costs today, what with inflation and all.) The convincer came for me when the same director let it be known that interns were more expendable than elevator operators. I took Horace Greeley's excellent advice and went west to Los Angeles County Hospital, where I was overjoyed to get $10 a month. What was so good about "the good old days?"

After an internship like that, plus a residency that was only little better paid, the doctor who hung out his own shingle could expect a long, slow period of sweating out a practice. Often he could not break even on living and office expenses in his first year of practice. It might be five years before he could expect to earn a fair living. Entering a group practice presented a most attractive alternative; he would have patients, a livable income, and financial security from the start. After years of slave labor, that was a dream come true.

Enthusiasts like to claim that there has been a fantastic rate of growth in group practice ever since those days, but such claims are not what they seem. A recent AMA report claimed that there were "40,000 physicians practicing full-time in more than 6000 groups"; others have claimed a "documented annual growth rate of 12 to 16 percent since the group practice movement began gathering full steam in 1946."

The trouble with those wild dreams is that the figures lump in with true groups all sorts of other medical partnerships. The AMA study made in 1970 could turn up only 24,000 physicians practicing in groups that offered diversified (comprehensive) care. These represent less than 10 percent of practicing physicians. A study that I made and published in *Medical Economics* in 1967 showed that from 1959 to 1966 the number of multispecialty groups increased by only 15 percent, while the number of single-specialty partnerships skyrocketed 630 percent. The prestigious American Association of Medical Clinics lists only 260 multispecialty groups on its roster—a far cry from the

"6000" groups bandied about by the group practice enthusiasts.

The growth of prepaid groups has been even more glacial than that of groups in general. The Kaiser plans have had the greatest growth of any, but they have enjoyed the advantage of operating in areas of skyrocketing population growth, the West Coast and Hawaii. Nationally our population has increased by about 25 million in the past decade, while prepaid groups have increased their enrollments by about a million. Under the auspices of the late Walter Reuther and his United Auto Workers, the Community Health Association was founded in 1960 with the expectation of attracting 400,000 members in Detroit, plus millions in other cities, but after a decade its enrollment was only 75,000, and the majority of union members have elected a fee-for-service insurance plan. A plan in Cleveland stumbled so badly that it had to be taken over by Kaiser.

There appear to be several reasons for this. As people grow more affluent and move to the suburbs, the central city prepaid clinic loses its appeal. Those who move out may be replaced by new center city residents, but the net growth is small.

Prepaid care is sometimes severely fragmented. A friend of mine who belongs to New York's HIP wanted a routine physical examination. Because his family doctor was present at the group center only in the afternoons, while the lab and x-ray room received patients only in the mornings, the patient had to start off with two separate visits to the center. Then he had to arrange appointments and make separate trips to see a surgeon for a proctoscopy, a cardiologist's assistant for an electrocardiogram, an eye man, and an ear man. This was topped off with a second visit to the family doctor for a report—a total of seven different visits in all for an ordinary check-up!

Finally there are widespread complaints that prepaid group care tends to be too impersonal, too mechanical. Every important element of California labor, including some unions that in other respects are constantly at each other's throats, has banded together in search of alternative health-care systems. They do not want to do away with Kaiser, but they do want their members to have choices. Thomas Moore, Jr., director of the all-union project, said, "Talking to Kaiser is like trying to organize Ma Bell. They're just so damn big. They build capital by overloading in favor of reserves, so people can't get into hospitals or see the doctors. Kaiser is going to meet their target if they have to walk over every member they've got. They haven't had to accommodate the consumer in years."

Many people believe that group practice, through its use of pooled resources and of paramedical personnel, can offer great cost savings. Here, again, I fear they are overly optimistic. In actual practice the savings tend to be relatively small. Such as they are, they tend to be put back into improvements of service or to redound to the benefit of the doctors rather than to bring about lower charges to patients. Group practice can offer a high quality of care, but not necessarily cheaper care.

Even the mighty Kaiser system, with all its advantages of huge scale, admits freely that savings on that account are relatively minor. Kaiser's lower total cost results almost entirely from fewer hospital admissions and fewer patient days as compared to surrounding areas generally. This is comparing apples to oranges. California, especially, abounds in numerous small, proprietary hospitals operating under standards that are mediocre or worse, and the costly, inferior care that they give distorts the general average. A more valid comparison would be between Kaiser and fee-for-service groups that maintain equally high standards. My experience leads me to believe that such a study would show that Kaiser has no cost advantage important enough to overcome the disadvantage of its less personal and often inconvenient care.

One other factor that militates against an extremely rapid growth of group practice is that this way of working has less financial lure for physicians than it once did. A young doctor who joins a group usually receives at first a smaller share than do the senior partners and is raised to their level only over a period of years. But young doctors are no longer paupers. An intern today earns, quite literally, more in a week than I earned per year. A "moonlighting" resident can earn more in a single twelve-hour period! The newly fledged resident can step at once into highly lucrative practice. In some specialties, notably radiology, offers to first-year men of $40,000 a year go begging. I have known doctors to open offices in advance of completing their residencies and to enter the first day of practice with appointment books filled for weeks ahead. Forty years ago a physician in his first five years of practice averaged about $5000 a year; today the *median income* is $34,000 a year, and almost one-third of beginning doctors net $40,000 or more. It is not easy for groups to meet this kind of competition; Kaiser sends recruiting teams out scouting the country for new doctors.

Group practice also has another kind of competition. Today the man who wants to practice high grade medicine tends to gravitate toward the medical schools, which are ever hungry for faculty talent. They can offer prestige and better research facilities, as well as good money.

All in all, while I am happy to see group practice encouraged by every feasible means, I expect its growth to continue to be steady rather than to zoom spectacularly. Our major selling point will continue to be high quality, not low cost.

7

THE PYRE IN THE WALDORF CELLAR

"IT looks as if society means to insist upon a more effective organization of medical services for all groups of people, upon distribution of costs of services over large numbers of families and individuals and upon making the prevention of disease a controlling purpose." Those prophetic words were spoken some forty years ago by George Vincent, president of the Rockefeller Foundation. Today he might delete the qualifications and say that society is *determined* upon those goals.

Yet our progress toward them has been painfully slow. On occasions we have even lost ground. Over the past decade, our relative position among the countries of the world has steadily declined as measured by such indicators as infant mortality and life expectancy. An American baby runs almost twice the risk of infant death as does a Swedish one. Our babies die at the rate of 22.1 per 1000 and Sweden's at 12.6. Not only can girl babies born in Norway and the Netherlands be expected to live longer than those born in the United States, but so can those born in Iceland and the Ukraine. You will look long and hard for any other standard-of-living index in which the United States does not stand number one. Why not in health?

The evolution of medical education in the United States has been a triumph; that of uniformly high quality health service, a disaster. Our medical care is a mixture of good and bad. In my own field of surgery, there is abundant evidence that the health-service machine is in dire need of an overhaul.

The harsh fact is that we have a double standard of surgical practice. Most patients are treated by conscientious, qualified, and ethical surgeons with therapeutic results that are impressive by any standard. In some specialized fields, American surgeons are universally recognized to be preeminent. It is for good reason that people come from all over the world to be treated at our great medical centers and clinics. Most surgical services are provided in well-regulated hospitals with excellent facilities. Satisfied patients express their gratitude in countless testimonials to doctors, hospital administrators, and nursing supervisors. Good hospitals that have surveyed their patients find that the pleased overwhelmingly outnumber the disgruntled. I would guess that thank-you letters to qualified surgeons and well-regulated hospitals outnumber malpractice suits by 1000 to 1. Some people actually become ecstatic over their medical care! Most of us recall how President Johnson, in a fit of enthusiasm over his gallbladder operation, ripped open his shirt to bare his scar to photographers so that the entire world could marvel at his surgeon's skill with a scalpel.

There is another and sordid side to the coin of surgical practice. A substantial number of patients are the victims of unnecessary and often clumsily performed operations by untrained, and thus unqualified, doctors. The unsuspecting public may be swindled through such unethical practices as fee splitting and "ghost surgery."

Fee splitting is a specialist's kickback paid to a doctor who refers a patient to him. It is illegal in some states and unethical in all. It is nonexistent in some places and common in others. In an article that appeared in *Medical Economics* in 1967, I wrote, "The fact remains that even in Chicago, the home city of the American College of Surgeons and the American Medical Association, fee splitting is rampant. Few young surgeons in Chicago would dream of starting practice without being fully prepared to split fees." The magazine reprinted that quotation three years later and added, "Not one voice of protest has been raised since that appeared in print." Fee splitting, of course, raises the cost of medical care, since the specialist must charge enough to cover not only his own services, but the kickback as well.

Ghost surgery is the substitution at the operating table, while the patient is unconscious, of another doctor for the one the patient believes is doing the operation. This unethical procedure is not to be confused with a senior resident doing all or part of an operation under qualified supervision. Ghost surgery is out-and-out deception. Mrs. Jones thinks that her family physician, Dr. Smith, is going to operate on her. Smith knows he is not qualified to do the operation, but he does not want to lose face by letting Mrs. Jones know it. He does the preoperative workup. The last thing Mrs. Jones sees as she slips under the anesthesia and the first thing she sees when she wakes up is his kindly face. In between Dr. Brown has come in, met the patient for the first and only time through a hole in the surgical drapes, done the job and departed. Naturally he and Smith split the latter's fee.

The main explanation for what is wrong with our surgical practice lies buried in history. Abraham Flexner uncontrovertibly documented in 1910 that the majority of doctors of the day were poorly educated and poorly trained. At the same time, dramatic advances were making it possible for surgeons to relieve suffering and cure diseases previously not amenable to surgery. As far back as 1894, a world-renowned surgeon, Dr. Nicholas Senn, was calling the attention of the medical profession to the fact that more progress had been made in surgical science in the preceding ten years than in the previous 100.

In the early years of this century, the need for well-trained surgeons far exceeded the supply. The inevitable result was a proliferation of charlatans and bunglers, because the public had no way of telling a qualified doctor from a quack. Dr. Thomas Mackenzie, in his 1911 presidential address to the New Jersey Medical Society, deplored the fact that the public could not "discriminate between the spurious and the genuine doctor of medicine any more than it could in 1776 when New Jersey was but a colony and quacks abounded like the locusts of Egypt."

The newly organized Congress of Surgeons of North America bethought itself in 1912 to do for hospital surgical practice what Flexner had done for medical schools. When the congress was succeeded by the American College of Surgeons in 1913, the new organization's first president, Dr. John Finney, announced that one of its major goals was to "educate the public up to the idea that there is a difference between the honest, conscientious, well-trained surgeon and the purely commercial operator."

With an initial grant of $30,000 from the Carnegie Foundation, the study got under way in 1916, headed by Dr. John Bowman, first director of the ACS. But there were two major differences from the Flexner study.

Flexner had been able to visit all the 155 existing medical schools; Bowman did not have the resources to cover 3000 hospitals and so had to limit himself to the 692 with 100 or more beds each, excluding smaller hospitals which could be expected to be less well-regulated. Secondly, Flexner was an outsider with no personal ties to the medical schools; the surgical study was conducted by surgeons who were appraising themselves and their colleagues. This was the beginning of "peer review" of which we shall see more later. The first difference was bad enough; the second was fatal.

From the start Bowman and his staff hit pay dirt, and dirt is the proper word. Most hospitals had no means of supervising or controlling their medical staffs and did not systematically check on the quality of the care being given. Medical records were generally shoddy, where they existed at all. X-ray and laboratory facilities were generally inadequate.

Bowman's staff, for example, compared the outcome of 100 cases of "chronic appendicitis" each at a "good" hospital and a "bad" one. (We may disregard the fact that a diagnosis of "chronic" appendicitis would *never* be made at a good hospital today.) At the good hospital, a complete history, physical examination, and blood count was recorded for all patients; at the poor hospital for only 14 percent of the patients. A working diagnosis before the operation and progress notes afterward were always charted at one hospital and never at the other. The infection rate at the poor hospital was 400 percent higher than at the other; the death rate 450 percent greater.

In sum the study found that the medical care being rendered at the time was adequate in only 89 of the 692 large hospitals. What it must have been like in most of the 2300 smaller ones is horrifying to think about. The shocking truth was that most hospitals were puspockets and that the then traditional American fear of hospitals was all too justified.

With this dynamite bomb in hand, the ACS had the weapon that should have enabled it to perform a Flexner-like service and force a revolution in hospital practice. But there was the fatal flaw of "peer review." Doctors had welcomed the Flexner report both altruistically because its effect was to improve the quality of care and selfishly because the closing of poor schools helped to lessen competition in a profession they regarded as overcrowded. Of course, the medical schools had no power to suppress Flexner.

But the ACS study hit the surgeons themselves, and the ACS did have the power to suppress its own document. With the impact of Flexner fresh in their minds, the surgeons correctly feared the consequences if the public should learn the truth. Vigorous measures were called for, and the surgeons, always activists, were equal to the occasion. Utterly contemptuous of the Carnegie Foundation mandate to publish the facts, the ACS, meeting in New York's Waldorf-Astoria Hotel in 1919, took a "public be damned" stance. They were not even content to file and forget the evidence because it might leak out later on. Instead they settled on cremation! The survey reports on the "bad" hospitals were resolutely carted to the Waldorf basement and burned forthwith. Evidently no vase was available; not even the ashes were saved.

The opportunity to save countless lives and prevent untold suffering went up in smoke on that fateful October day. Surgery has never recovered from that act of intellectual and moral cowardice. The objectionable surgical practices that some patients must contend with today may be said to continue to exist simply because the leaders of surgery, with the power in their hands, threw away a golden opportunity to force the establishment of strict controls over commercially minded operators and inferior hospitals. The hospital accreditation program that the ACS had established in the previous year has not been an acceptable substitute, as I shall show in a later chapter. Surgical practice was left unregulated, and unfortunately we are still plagued by this lack of control. This has made it possible for two distinctly different schools of surgery to evolve. Most surgeons are trained in hospital-based programs that meet standards set by the AMA and by the American Board of Surgery, and they must pass stiff examinations based upon that training in order to be certified. But there are no legal requirements that they do this.

A smaller number of physicians choose to enter practice as soon as they can win state licensure, which is usually at the end of the internship year. They may then, quite legally, operate upon patients, even though they have had no surgical training or supervision. Nothing prevents these people from listing themselves in the Yellow Pages as surgeons. They are surgeons by self-proclamation.

A state license confers unlimited rights to practice medicine and surgery, even though the examinations are meant only to determine a physician's general medical knowledge at the internship level. In no state do the examiners pass judgment on a physician's skill in the operating room, or for that matter, in the practice of any other specialty.

Our soldiers, sailors, and airmen are assured of skilled surgery because military surgeons are strictly classified according to training and ability. Veterans are similarly protected at the hospitals of the Veterans Administration. Needless to say, at well-regulated civilian hospitals, operating room privileges are not granted to the untrained. Unfortunately these strictures do not prevent self-proclaimed surgeons from wielding a busy scalpel. Doctors who would be deemed unqualified at our better hospitals operate with impunity in civilian hospitals with inferior standards.

Ordinarily, reputable surgeons operate at reputable hospitals, nonsurgeons at disreputable places, but this rule has some exceptions. It is not uncommon for hospitals that have raised their standards and now scrutinize closely the credentials of all new doctors to have a few old practitioners who have had operating privileges for many years and who, for sympathetic reasons, are allowed to retain them. I wonder how the medical profession would feel about flying if an airline were to say something like this: "At least 90 percent of our pilots are fully qualified to fly modern jets. We do have a few fellows who've been with us since the days of the Ford Trimotor and who don't understand much about the newer planes, but whom we keep on for old times' sake. Don't worry about them, though. They'll all be dying off in the next ten or fifteen years." A doctor who puts a patient on the operating table assumes a responsibility for that patient's life, just as does a pilot who takes people up in the air.

Just how prevalent is bad surgery? There are no exact statistics, of course, but indirect evidence gives a strong indication. Consider the removal of tonsils. More than a million tonsillectomies are performed in this country each year, making this operation the one most frequently done by far. Are all these operations necessary? One doubts it when one learns that Swedish children lose their tonsils only one-tenth as often as American children. As a British cynicism has it: "One cannot avoid the conclusion that there is a tendency for the operation to be performed as a routine prophylactic ritual for no particular reason and with no particular result." However, there is a particular result for more than 300 children each year: they die! Can this be related to the fact that only 25 percent of the tonsillectomies performed in this country are done by physicians with special expertise in diseases of the ear, nose, and throat?

Here are some interesting comparisons. Under the Medicaid program in California, tonsillectomies are performed on children below the age of sixteen almost twice as often as under some Blue Shield plans. Even more astonishing is the comparison with some group practice clinics. Such clinics, in the main, provide a high quality of care because the member doctors are continually examining each other's work with the acute awareness that one incompetent member could damage the good name of the whole group. The medically indigent children of California are having their tonsils removed at a *ten times higher* rate than are the patients at some group practice clinics which take care of nonindigent children. I am being conservative in suggesting, then, that we could greatly lower the incidence of tonsillectomy without damaging the health of American children.

Eliminating wretched practices is, of course, only the first step in elevating overall medical care quality. The next logical move would be the investigation of poor care. For example, GPs are not the only ones prone to operation overuse. Indeed, the California statistics are not sophisticated enough to indicate whether GPs or ENT specialists are guilty of the exceedingly high tonsillectomy rate on Medicaid patients in this state.

The tonsillectomy problem has other ramifications. Some pediatricians with busy private practices refer only five or six patients a year for a tonsillectomy and have just as good results as other pediatricians who refer ten times that many. Some pediatricians even do their own tonsillectomies and coincidentally (perhaps?) find the operation indicated disturbingly often.

To pursue the overutilization issue further, how many ENT men perform a tonsillectomy too often because they do not want to tell the parents that the referring doctor erred in the first place by stating that the child needed his tonsils removed? Could this also explain why the incidence of appendectomies varies markedly from one surgeon to another? Granted that trained surgeons operate better than untrained ones, specialists as well as GPs have quality care questions that should be resolved. The problem of the well-performed but still unnecessary operation permeates the entire field of surgery.

More can be learned from the hospital experience of well-regulated, prepaid, closed-panel group practice plans. Members of such plans show from 30 percent to 50 percent lower hospital utilization and surgical rates than do patients with ordinary health insurance. The differences are especially marked in those areas where unnecessary surgery is most frequently seen—tonsillectomies, appendectomies, and "female" operations. The reasons are two:

in well-regulated programs, such as the Kaiser Foundation Health plan, surgeons do not benefit financially from operating on any particular patient, and the quality of care is rigidly controlled, with only bona fide surgeons permitted to wield the knife. Note that I have said "well-regulated" plans. There are no fewer than 50 prepaid health-care service plans registered in California. Like solo practitioners, some are excellent; some are very far from that.

Still further evidence of the prevalence of poor surgical practices can be found in data of the United Mine Workers Welfare and Retirement Fund. When the fund adopted a policy permitting only qualified surgeons to operate upon its beneficiaries, the rate of surgery dropped precipitously within 90 days. It has remained about 50 percent lower than it was under the old policy. When the fund adopted strict standards concerning the indications for tonsillectomy, the drop was even more dramatic. By one simple action, the UMW improved the quality of medical care rendered to its beneficiaries and made substantial savings in costs. It merely eliminated operations by a type of physician whom I consider to be a menace—the untrained GP surgeon.

Most general practitioners well deserve the confidence of their patients because they seek consultation when a problem arises that is beyond their competence. The GP's aim is "to engage in medical and surgical procedures for which he is qualified by training and experience," and I enjoy excellent relationships with those who follow that rule. But GPs, like other people, are subject to the usual human frailties, and some of them are undermining public confidence in medicine.

I write these words fully aware that there will be shrill denunciations of any strictures that would reduce the GP's operating privileges. There are GPs who would like to operate more, not less. Under the old rule that the best defense is a good offense, the California Academy of General Practice has come out in favor of "*increasing* the surgical emphasis in general practice." Many California GPs can certainly do so if they want to, for they are subject to little outside control. A recent poll of the CAGP showed that 93 percent of its members belong to hospitals that allow them to do everything they consider themselves qualified to do. That number undoubtedly includes many GPs who recognize the limitations of their qualifications, but it also includes others who do not.

There is practically nothing that some general practitioners consider themselves unqualified to do, including formidable operations that would tax the skills of the most eminent surgeons in the country. Even without formal training, some physicians develop a modest proficiency in the technical aspects of surgery, and a few become good operators. More often they flounder around the abdomen like a fish out of water.

Not only their technique, but their judgment frequently leaves much to be desired. I have known GPs to remove a woman's uterus to cure headaches and constipation. Worse, I have known of a case where biopsy examination showed the patient to have a malignancy in the lower part of the uterus and where the doctor removed only the upper part, leaving the cancer behind.

Consider the uterine suspension, in which the doctor takes a uterus that is tipped backward in the body and attaches it to the anterior wall, an operation a specialist rarely recommends. You could examine the operating room schedules of good hospitals for years without finding one listed. Yet I have known GPs to do this operation on teenagers as young as fourteen to cure irregular menses! In some "Mickey Mouse" hospitals, such operations are scheduled quite frequently.

I know of a GP who, on his first attempt to do a gallbladder operation, used as his only assistant another GP who had never done one either! The result was disastrous, and when the patient became jaundiced, yet a third GP attempted to rectify the damage—again unsuccessfully. Needless to say, none of these abuses would have been condoned in a reputable hospital.

I could fill many more pages with equally incredible experiences, and I am not alone in observing these surgical indignities; many other surgeons can tell similar stories.

How, you may ask, is it possible that unqualified doctors can obtain hospital privileges? Some hospitals are just plain lax about whom they will give surgical privileges to and about what those doctors then do. This tends especially to be the case in proprietary hospitals, which are profit-making and privately owned, often by the very doctors who make up its staff. It may also be the case with small community (nonprofit) hospitals, where the few doctors must work closely together and are reluctant to criticize one of their number. (This is not to disparage all hospitals in either class; there are excellent hospitals in both groups.)

When a group of California general practitioners was denied operating privileges at other hospitals, the doctors opened their own "GP-run" institution and now decide for themselves who is qualified to do what. There is nothing mysterious about the way they reach this decision: an article in *Medical Economics* describes it in all its simplicity:

> A young GP I'll call "Dr. Sherwood" applied for T. & A. [removal of tonsils and adenoids] privileges some months ago at [a] Hospital. . . . The hospital's credentials committee authorized him to perform three T. & A.s under the monitoring of other staff doctors. Each of the supervising doctors presented a report that satisfied the credentials committee, and the hospital granted "Dr. Sherwood" his T. & A. privileges. . . . The cornerstone of its achievement is its policy of awarding privileges to the "Dr. Sherwoods" *on a basis of demonstrated competence* (italics mine).

There you have it! "Dr. Sherwood" performed three T & As and he is proclaimed competent. A few questions come to mind. Did the patients need the T & As in the first place? Would "Dr. Sherwood" be able to handle a post-operative tonsillar bed hemorrhage? Were the three general practitioners who judged Dr. Sherwood's competence themselves competent to make that judgment? If "Dr. Sherwood" had proved incompetent and a tragedy resulted, which one of the judges would be appointed to explain the "monitoring" system to the distraught parents of the child?

Even more interesting questions might be asked of those who go a step further and condone the performance of "simple" operations, like appendectomies and hernia repairs, by GPs. But most thought-provoking of all is the passionate insistence by some untrained GP surgeons that they be permitted to do gallbladder operations, radical surgery for cancer of the breast, and even more difficult operations on the thyroid, stomach, and colon. It is estimated that more than one million *major* operations are performed by GPs every year.

Perhaps the height of fatuity and lack of understanding was reached by a nonphysician who claimed in his book a few years ago that "even much uncomplicated major surgery can be handled by general practitioners." Who can tell beforehand which major operation will turn out not to be complicated? Even experienced surgeons may operate for what they think is simple appendicitis, only to find a much more complicated problem when the abdomen is opened. In this situation an untrained physician can only attempt an operation he is unqualified to perform or close the patient and call for help. Neither of these choices is fair to the patient. There is a form of hernia called a sliding hernia which is very difficult to repair, even in the best of hands. The rate of recurrence is always fairly high; when GPs attempt the operation, the rate of recurrence becomes prohibitive. I have seen these hernias recur before the patient even left the hospital. Before the stitches were removed, the bulges were back. Unqualified surgeons took chances that they would be able to handle whatever arose, but it was not the doctor who stood to lose. It was the patient.

People who write about surgical technique should take the time to consult surgeons. They would learn that there is a vast difference between a surgeon and one who operates. Many doctors can learn in fairly short order the mechanical techniques of performing a T & A and a number of other operations; such a doctor is an operator. But a surgeon, in addition to being technically skilled, must have special diagnostic abilities, a thorough knowledge of pre- and postoperative care, and the judgement and competence to handle the unexpected problems that so often arise. These skills can only be developed by a properly supervised residency training program. There are no short-cuts to becoming a surgeon. Surgeons alone—not oper-ators—should be operating on people.

Some of the more aggressive general practitioner sur-geons took a really bold step a few years ago. Two GPs and a few of their *layman* friends incorporated the Ameri-can Society of Abdominal Surgeons and issued certificates of membership. The society actually gained official status of a kind through the AMA. The AMA membership is divided into sections, according to specialty, but the mem-ber himself chooses the section to which he wishes to be-long. At the 1968 AMA convention, the society packed the meeting of the surgical section with its own members and elected its own slate of officers. (Happily the trained surgeons regained control the following year.) The group continues in business, and many a GP sports on his office wall an impressive certificate denoting membership in the American Society of Abdominal Surgeons. The public is totally unaware that the certificate may have been issued to a phyisician who has never had anywhere near the formal training in surgery required by the American Board of Surgery.

The flagrantly bad medical practices that I have de-scribed show few signs of abating and may even increase. The country is presently seeing a spate of construction of new, small, proprietary hospitals, many of which are re-turning handsome dividends to their stockholders. As noted, there are excellent ones among them, but in many the question must arise whether the greater concern of the entrepreneurs is for quality medical care or for profit.

For those who are apathetic or calloused, the problem of the GP-surgeon will solve itself in time: the general practitioner will be phased out of medical practice in thirty or forty years. But those of us who are concerned with life and limb now are not willing to wait that long. We want higher standards of medical quality now. The first step toward getting it is to decide what "medical care quality" means.

8

LUXURY CARE MAY NOT
BE QUALITY CARE

> If the doctor shall open an abscess with a bronze knife
> and shall kill the patient, or shall destroy the sight of his
> eye, his hand shall be cut off.
>
> Code of Hammurabi

SINCE the days of ancient Babylon, people have cared deeply about the quality of medical care. Twentieth-century Americans are closer to the Babylonians than may seem likely at first glance. True, we are concerned about much more than merely whether the patient died or went blind, but we always end up with the same question: Did the patient receive the proper treatment? Even the extreme punishments we mete out are fundamentally similar: lifting a doctor's license to practice or withdrawing his hospital privileges amounts to cutting off his professional "hands."

One cannot go to a conference on health care today without hearing endless talk about the *quality* of care. It is the underlying theme at every meeting, whether the topic under discussion is how health services can be better organized and distributed or how much they cost. We are told that the primary responsibility for health care rests with the professionals who render it, and it is up to them to achieve and maintain high *quality*; that hospital effectiveness must be increased and costs cut, without sacrifice of *quality*; that the system must be reshaped while we "close the *quality* gap."

This emphasis on quality is certainly justified. Our society has awakened to the speciousness of the claims of organized medicine that medical care in the United States is "unsurpassed elsewhere in the world" and that this care is enjoyed by "greater numbers of our citizens and in greater proportion than citizens of any other nation." The latter statement is patently false, as WHO statistics demonstrate. The former is true only for Americans at the top end of the health-care spectrum; it is certainly not true for millions at the bottom.

Physicians have come a long way since King Hammurabi's law decreed that they should literally lose their appendages for untoward operative results. In today's hospital it is not a Babylonian executioner with an ax who looks over the surgeon's shoulder, but a group of his fellow doctors. In medical matters the profession is privileged to regulate itself. In most hospitals self-discipline works well enough, but is "most" good enough? I think not.

Public patience with medicine's inadequacies has been taxed to the breaking point. Posing the problem in platitudes is no longer acceptable. An AMA president recently stated, "All of us agree that we must do a better job in many areas of the country to make certain that everyone, regardless of his financial status, has high quality care available to him." Indeed, we do agree, but how far is medicine prepared to go to bring about this "high quality care?"

And what *is* high quality care? At the three-day 1968 National Health Forum on "Quality in Health Care," the definition proved to be discouragingly elusive. It does not seem to me to be all that elusive, as I shall show. I think the medical profession would like to believe that it is elusive so that it cannot be pinned down. The conference took a multidimensional approach to its topic, thus answering the query in the title of the chairman's concluding address, "Quo Vadis?" Nowhere! The forum was less interested in the quality of medical care than in the "quality of life itself," and such matters as social values, community values, and citizen responsibility all came in for their due share of banal discussion.

One psychiatrically oriented pundit, Roslyn Lindheim, an architect, proclaimed that poor quality medical care could result from "motel lobby" furniture in the doctor's waiting room because sterile interior decoration could generate hostility in the patient! Piffle! Doctors usually have commonsense about these matters. They know who their patients are and furnish their waiting rooms accordingly. The Park Avenue physician who serves mostly millionaires will obviously have a far different waiting room than the small town doctor whose practice is mainly among mill hands. Even if the patient of one strayed into the waiting room of the other and felt somewhat out of place, no great harm would be done. What happens in the treatment room is what *really* counts.

The same authority also questioned the clustering of doctors' offices near hospitals: "The proximity of office and hospital reduces the amount of travel time required (by the doctor). This arrangement may be the most effective grouping for the doctors, but is it most effective grouping for the patient?" As far as the patient's travel time is concerned, no, it is not the most effective grouping. But so what? The patient comes to my office relatively rarely and to the hospital even more rarely. I go to my office every day and make hospital rounds at least once, and usually twice, daily. In an emergency I may have to leave a waiting room full of patients and rush to the hospital. Is travel time more important for the patient or for the doctor? Which grouping of office and hospital is most effective for high quality care?

There are plenty of definitions of high quality care. One of the damndest comes from a medical school professor whose name I mercifully omit:

> High-quality patient care and community health services involve the use of sound principles and practices of management for the co-ordinated application of the proper space and modern technological equipment with the available physicians and ancillary medical personnel having skills and talents, as taught by the recognized leaders of the profession at the given time, so as to provide the patient with maximum availability of medical services which conform to established standards for professional proficiency and efficient fiscal administration.

I do not see that it is any more difficult to define high quality care than to define high quality automobiles. The dictionary defines "quality" as the goodness or badness of something, the degree of excellence. These, of course, are comparatives, meaningless without standards by which to judge. A Cadillac can only be called a high quality automobile by comparison with inferior makes; if there were no other cars but Cadillacs, you could not call one either a good or a bad car. Similarly, the United States has higher quality health care than Peru or Tanganyika, but lower than Sweden. The affluent residents of Westchester County, New York, generally get better quality medical care than the abjectly poor, rural slum dwellers of Harlan County, Kentucky. A look at the objective statistics would convince anyone that these conclusions are irrefutable.

So I take issue with Dr. Dwight L. Wilbur, former AMA president, who told that organization's Third National Conference on the Socioeconomics of Health Care, "There are as many definitions of 'quality' as there are people in this room. The answer is purely subjective." The figures on such matters as infant mortality, the incidence of disease, or the comparative death rate in different hospitals among patients undergoing the same operations are hardly subjective, and they show quite clearly the low quality of care in Appalachia and in city slums. That may be understandable, if not forgivable, in view of the poverty in those places, but what is not so understandable is why our mainstream health services are of lower quality than those of other advanced countries.

The answer, I submit, is that we have not focused sharply enough on the essential element of quality. For example, the 1968 National Health Forum listed seven correlates of quality: availability, accessibility, competence of manpower, continuity, responsiveness, individualization, and comprehensiveness. Certainly all these are factors in establishing the degree of excellence of care, but by no means should they be weighted equally.

Even chiropractors and other quacks offer many of these correlates to their unfortunate victims. The patient in the private room of a plush community hospital, with his color TV, telephone at hand, and carpeted floor, may enjoy six

out of the seven *and still receive low quality care.* The
patient in the overcrowded ward of the municipal hospital
may enjoy care of higher quality, even though he has had
to travel a long way to get there, must share a lavatory
with six others, and has to wait longer for his pain-relieving
medication because there are not enough nurses on duty.
If he has had the services of qualified surgeons, and the
private patient has not, he is getting care of better quality.
All the other factors are of small importance if competence
of the physician is lacking. All the correlates are desirable,
but there is no substitute for *competence.*

The competence of physicians can be measured, though
not always with the precision that we can measure the
competence of baseball players. If two ball players have
batting averages of .310 and .225, respectively, we have no
trouble forming a solid opinion as to which is the better
performer at the plate. A very few such standards can be
applied to medicine. If the patients in one hospital con-
tract infections three times as often as do the patients in
another, it is pretty clear which is the cleaner place. If
two surgeons repair hernias, and if 2 percent of Dr. A's
patients suffer recurrences while 20 percent of Dr. B's do,
it is also pretty clear which man is more skilled at that
operation. While their professional colleagues may be
aware of the two doctors' respective "batting averages,"
unfortunately patients are not. If they were, Dr. B would
probably get no more patients with hernias, and a good
thing that would be, too.

Standards as sharp as that, however, are not commonly
possible to measure the competence of a highly complex
profession. But despite that lack, medical care can be
classified into such broad categories as poor, good, and

superior, and the profession knows how to do it. (If anesthetists could only tell all they know about surgeons!) The profession acknowledges the advanced training and increased competence of specialists who are members of the official specialty boards, and there are still more honors available in the various branches of medicine to doctors of superior attainment. For example, to qualify for the American Academy of General Practice a doctor must demonstrate that he is keeping up to date by taking at least fifty hours of continuing education courses a year. There can be no question that the man who has that certificate (or the diploma of the American Board of Family Practice) hanging on his office wall is more competent than the GP who is unable to qualify for it.

(Incidentally, if you want to find out the professional qualifications of your particular doctor, these are matters of public knowledge. The AMA publishes a directory of MDs, arranged geographically by state and community. It gives such information as where the doctor went to medical school, where he took his internship and residency, if any, his specialty board and professional societies, and whether or not he is on a medical school faculty. A copy of this directory may usually be consulted at the office of your county medical society.)

Experience has shown that it is much easier to pick the relatively few bad apples out of the professional barrel than it is to grade the fine differences between the good and the better ones. It follows from this that the quickest way we can raise the general quality of health care in this country is not by pursuing the elusive, less worrisome distinctions between good quality and superior quality care, but by getting rid of poor quality care altogether. I contend that poor quality care is so prevalent that it deserves to become our prime target. It is all very well for the medical staff of a first-rate hospital to work hard at self-improvement, and I am all for it. But we would accomplish a lot more for the general level of care if we zeroed in on the poor medical practices at low-grade hospitals.

Let me make clear the distinction between *quality* and *equality* of care. Short 50,000 doctors as we are, and lacking the compulsory powers of a socialized system to prevent physicians from practicing where they please, we cannot possibly in the immediate future offer the 30 million medically indigent Americans the same luxuries that are available to their more affluent countrymen. Until we solve our fundamental problems, the poor will continue to fly economy class on the health-service plane, while the wealthier ones in first class will continue to enjoy the free martinis and more individual attention from the stewardess. But the difference between a wide seat and steak on the one hand and a narrow seat and chicken on the other is of secondary importance. What matters most is that the same qualified pilot be flying both sections of the plane. If we cannot offer the poor *equality* of care for the time being, a minimum *quality* of care is their fundamental right. The affluent and sophisticated should not fly in a well-maintained plane with a capable crew on the flight deck while the poor and unsophisticated take their chances in a rickety crate with an unqualified pilot.

In an article in *Esquire* (October 1968), Fred Powledge asked, "What will the doctors do for Jean Paul Getty that they won't do for you?" Plenty! They will arrange for a private suite in the hospital, order special nurses around the clock, and see to it that Mr. Getty gets the stock quotations on closed circuit television. But the doctors cannot remove his appendix more skillfully, prescribe a more effective antibiotic for his pneumonia, or transfuse him with purer blood if his ulcer bleeds than they can for the poorest of patients. No, good doctors do not use dull knives on the poor as Mr. Powledge has intimated.

As a matter of plain fact, there are many instances where I myself would much rather be treated in a large county hospital than in many community hospitals. If I were severely burned, if my liver were damaged in an automobile accident, if I suffered a gunshot wound, I would far prefer to be in the county hospital, which is geared to handle such problems, than in the average community hospital, which is not.

It is a sad fact that when it comes to judging the quality of care, most Americans are babes in the medical woods. They tend to judge a doctor by his suave manner and a hospital by its amenities and are no more capable of choosing a highly qualified physician than I am of selecting a high grade diamond. Nor does one have to be poor to be medically unsophisticated. A famous Hollywood star thought he was buying the best care when his fashionable doctor put him into an expensive proprietary hospital. The patient never knew his operation was performed by a "ghost."

Members of minority groups often make emotional rather than reasoned choices. Some black people are satisfied only when their doctors are black; some Latins do not want to be treated by a gringo. In point of fact, some of the worst medicine that I know of is practiced by minority group physicians who exploit unsophisticated members of their own ethnic group. I know of black physicians who practice "shotgun medicine," bringing their black patients back week after week for costly but unnecessary injections. I know Mexican-American surgeons who specialize in unnecessary operations performed upon their non-English-speaking neighbors. The correlation between competence and skin color is exactly nil: there are good and bad doctors in every ethnic group.

At present both rich and poor suffer from low quality medical care. It is a matter for national concern. Removing glands from the neck to cure bronchial asthma is as useless in North Carolina as it is in Massachusetts. Ghost surgery is as despicable in Illinois as in California. A great many of the 15 million operations performed annually in the United States are unnecessary or poorly performed; the cost in human suffering is very high indeed.

So long as these practices go on, the United States as a nation can never hope to reach the level of surgical practice that England and Sweden have attained. British standards are higher and their results are better despite the fact that half their hospitals were built in the nineteenth century and would long since have been condemned in this country. Toilet facilities may be primitive, but surgical results are superb. The thing that counts most is professional competence. Surgery at well-regulated American hospitals takes second place to none the world over. The difference is that the British and Swedes insist on high standards at all their hospitals.

We do not.

9

WHO WATCHES THE WATCHDOG?

QUESTION: Who is the public's watchdog over the medical profession? Answer: the medical profession. Most of the time the system works well enough, but where human life is at stake *most of the time* is not good enough. Rather we need a system that, as nearly as human frailty permits, will work *all the time*. To use my airline analogy again, we would not dream of permitting a system of pilot selection that worked only most of the time. Stringent Government regulation and high airline standards aim to see that every time he takes over the controls of an airliner, a man is highly skilled, fully trained, cold sober, and not likely to pop a heart valve in mid-flight. The system works to an astonishing degree. Pilots, being as human as doctors, no doubt do make some errors in spite of every safeguard, but I have yet to hear of a U.S. jetliner crashing because the man up front was trained to fly only piston-engined aircraft.

Why should we demand less of a man who is licensed to use a knife on another human being? An incompetent shoe salesman who misfits me may cause a few blisters which I can remedy by not wearing his shoes, but an incompetent surgeon can cause serious suffering, crippling, even death. On *any* U. S. airline, *every* passenger is guaranteed a given level of competence on the flight deck. What controls do we need to insure that *every* patient will be guaranteed the same level of competence at *any* hospital?

Let us look at such controls as now exist, starting at the top, the national level. Federal law imposes two principal conditions that may be regarded as impinging on the quality of medical care, both enacted as part of the amendments to the Social Security Act that created Medicare. The first states that any hospital that has the approval of the Joint Commission on Accreditation of Hospitals is automatically elegible to receive Medicare funds. (We shall see how meaningful such accreditation is shortly.) Nonaccredited hospitals may also receive Medicare money if they are approved for the purpose by their respective states.

Federal law also requires hospitals taking Medicare patients to have utilization review committees of their medical staffs. These committees are supposed to examine the admissions of Medicare patients to make sure that hospitalization was required and to check the case again from time to time to make sure that the patient's continued stay is necessary. As far as the law is concerned, the purpose of the committees is economic, not medical. Their aim is to protect the Government against paying for unnecessary hospital care. There is no requirement that they concern themselves with the quality of that care.

Though the bitterness of the AMA's fight against Medicare will be long remembered, and though many of its leaders viewed utilization review with the darkest suspicion, the organization has now found that this particular bugaboo was only a butterfly. It is, after all, only a matter of the doctors of a hospital judging themselves. It was not as though the Federal Government were attempting to impose "coercive national standards," as an AMA past president, Dr. Dwight L. Wilbur, feared. "Attempts to impose standards on a national scale in such a personal matter as patient care are to be condemned," Dr. Wilbur went on. "The intangible but necessary ingredient of professional judgment does not lend itself to standardization."

No meeting of the AMA in recent years has been without a full quota of fulsome praise for the concept of peer review, by which the AMA means that organized medicine, and only organized medicine, shall have any voice in judging a doctor's professional conduct. What is more, though the AMA may hand down some general principles of ethics, often clouded with such vagueness as to be virtually meaningless, the question of taking any specific action upon those principles is to be left to the physicians of a local community. The organization will not set "coercive national standards" even for itself. How the quality of care is to be assessed on any level, local or national, without objective stands is never explained. The AMA merely shuts off all argument by pompously proclaiming that American medicine is already "the best in the world." The AMA has never hesitated to flail lustily away at such non-MD quacks as chiropractors, and it has even cautiously seen fit "to safeguard and inform the medical profession and the public with respect to the treatment of obesity." Are obesity doctors more dangerous than untrained surgeons? Obviously not.

Is there any more effective control at the state level?

The answer is an almost unqualified no. The states do license doctors to practice medicine. The license is usually granted at the end of the internship year after the physician has passed an examination. (In eleven states, not even an internship year is required!) All it does is to insure that the doctor has a minimum of basic knowledge and is of reasonably good character at that time. He can retain that license for the rest of his life without ever opening another book, attending a single medical meeting, or learning one new fact. His license is *unrestricted*, giving him the legal right to do anything he pleases in medicine and surgery. In the privileges it bestows, the license makes no distinction between the rawest recruit fresh out of internship and the outstanding professor-specialists at the medical school. Anything the one may do legally, the other may also do. Licensing laws offer no protection whatever against the doctor who attempts something beyond his competence.

Moreover, the degree of competence required to obtain a license varies enormously from state to state. The failure rate on state licensure examinations ranges from zero to 62 percent. In 1968 eight states failed more than 40 percent of the physician candidates, but seven other states failed none at all.

Licenses, once granted, can be revoked, but this is done very rarely indeed, and almost never unless the doctor has been openly convicted of some crime. In some states no license has been revoked within the memory of living man. In the few cases where licenses have been revoked, the offense has almost never been medical. Usually, it is moral, as in the occasional instances where doctors have been convicted of trafficking in narcotics, of sex offenses with patients, or of criminal abortion. In two nationally notorious cases, the offense was murder.

Since the profession likes to boast that doctors police doctors, do state medical societies do the job? They do not. Like the AMA, they are lavish in their praise of peer review, and also like the AMA they leave it to the county medical societies. With few exceptions the state society becomes involved only when there is an appeal from the decision of a county society. At the 1970 convention of the New York State society much was made of peer review, but when the officers held a news conference and the newspaper and broadcast reporters pressed them for some concrete instances of what had been done, the officers were unable to come up with a single example of self-policing by the association.

Dr. Warren F. Draper, former executive director of the United Mine Workers Welfare and Retirement Fund, tells of a doctor in another state who was found guilty of ghost surgery and fee splitting. He was also performing much unnecessary surgery—75 percent of the appendixes he removed were found to be perfectly normal. His punishment was a one-day suspension from his practice, and even the fact of that was to be kept confidential! All he had to do was take a day off and go fishing to "pay the penalty." What happened to the patients he treated thereafter is unrecorded.

At one time I was naive enough to think that those who pay so many of our hospital and doctor bills, the health insurers, might be interested in lowering premium rates by imposing stricter controls on surgical practices. I put my views to a meeting of half a dozen claim experts, representing the largest health insurance firms in southern

California. They all threw up their hands in defeat: "If medicine can't control professional competence, how can we?" Even Blue Cross swivel-hips the problem. Walter J. McNerney, president of the Blue Cross Association, has urged "caution" and expressed reservations about extending hospitalization review to encompass the quality of medical care. He says that physicians must "deal with individual problems [of quality] on a case-by-case basis."

The buck is passed down to the individual hospital and to the county medical society, but, unlike Harry Truman, they do not usually say that it stops here. Many half-informed people think that hospital accreditation by the Joint Commission on Accreditation of Hospitals is a guarantee of high quality medical practice. That impression is totally false, and the JCAH itself makes no such claim. Dr. John D. Porterfield, JCAH director, says the commission's aim is to "*foster the optimum environment* for the practice of high quality medicine. Dealing only with the environment has made some people mad at us, yet how can we approach medical care quality directly? We wouldn't be caught dead—or we'd be dead if caught—saying, 'You made the wrong decision, Doctor.' We hope the medical audit committee will say that, but we can't."

The JCAH traces its ancestry back to the hospital inspection program set up in 1918 by the American College of Surgeons and which led a year later to the incineration scene in the Waldorf basement. The ACS paid for the inspection program out of its own treasury, but over the years and after an outlay of more than $2 million, the burden grew too heavy. So the ACS successfully sought the help of other organizations; the Joint Commission was formed in 1952, beginning its own accreditation program the following year. The JCAH is now sponsored by four medical power blocs: the AMA and the American Hospital Association, each of which appoints seven commissioners, and the ACS and the American College of Physicians, each of which names three. Since 1966, when the commission began accrediting nursing homes, the American Association of Homes for the Aging and the American Nursing Home Association have been participating members, naming one commissioner each. The commission's roster is made up overwhelmingly of MDs.

Under the old ACS program, high standards were set for medical care quality. As David W. Stickney, associate director of the Illinois Hospital Association, put it, "Back in the 1930s accreditation stood for excellence well above the average. The ACS was quite satisfied if 25 percent or 30 percent of hospitals won it. It was *accreditation*, not just licensure."

This has not been true under the JCAH whose standards were, as Dr. Porterfield freely says, the "minimum essential." To upgrade those standards to "optimum achievable," the JCAH rewrote its rule book in 1970 and tightened its procedures, but it has not changed its fundamental philosophy, which is to create the environment and let the doctors live in it.

Here is how the system works: a hospital that wants to be accredited and believes that it can meet the JCAH published standards must make a written request for a survey. (The commission hates the word "inspection" because it sounds too much like policing.) The visit is then made by a team of two or three surveyors, depending on the hospital's size, one of whom is always an MD. Part of the survey is devoted to housekeeping matters, making sure that certain minimum facilities are there and in good order, such as checking on the cleanliness of kitchens and operating rooms and on methods of waste disposal.

Another part of the survey is devoted to the medical side, and here there is an iron insistence on accurate and complete medical records. There are two chief reasons for this. One is that such records are essential to the hospital's defense should a malpractice suit or other legal action be brought against it. The second is to provide that optimum environment in which the doctors can judge each other.

This is accomplished chiefly through three committees, which were mandatory under the old JCAH standards. (Under the 1970 rules, the number of committees is not spelled out; the hospital may have any number it chooses, so long as the necessary functions are performed.) The three are the utilization review committee, on which we have already touched, the tissue committee, and the medical audit committee.

The tissue committee receives reports from the pathologist on all tissue removed in surgery and reviews the appropriateness of various operations. For example, are surgeons removing too many normal appendixes? Every surgeon will remove some normal appendixes because the diagnosis of appendicitis cannot be made with 100 percent accuracy, and it is safer to remove a normal appendix occasionally than to allow a diseased one to burst. Inevitably in some cases the surgeon will be wrong. It is when the percentage of normal appendixes gets too high that the tissue committee becomes concerned.

In like fashion the medical audit committee studies cases from the medical, as opposed to the surgical, side of the hospital to determine whether or not the doctors there are acting properly. In addition, each department of the hospital—surgery, obstetrics, internal medicine, and so forth—is supposed to hold a monthly meeting of all doctors in that department. At these meetings, half a dozen representative cases are discussed. Did the doctor handle this case well, and if so what can the rest of us learn from him? Did he handle it badly, and if so what can the rest of us teach him?

To be performed properly, all these functions are dependent upon accurate and complete medical records. The reviewing doctors usually depend entirely on the records for their information, unless some point is unclear and it is necessary to call in the physician on the case for questioning. That is how good records create that optimum environment, and in our better hospitals the system works quite well. Under this constant scrutiny, good doctors become superior doctors, and a poor doctor can be quickly spotted and either brought up to par or have his privileges curtailed.

But the best tool in the world is of no value unless there is a willing hand to pick it up and use it. Flawless records are of minimum value if the medical staff of a hospital is not prepared to make good use of them. Dr. Porterfield recognized this when he said, "You can be a slob in a palace. We examine the palace on the theory that it produces the best conditions for good medical practice, but we say, 'You, the medical staff, must evaluate the work you do in it.'"

By these remarks I in no way intend to denigrate the value of the JCAH. The biennial visits of its surveyors and the internal audits of the hospital committees do help to improve medical care. I am aware of one hospital, admittedly a poor one to start with, where the mere institution of a tissue committee brought about a 50 percent decrease over a four-year period in the number of normal appendixes removed. I heartily agree with the basic philosophy of audits and have no sympathy for any hospital that balks at inspection of its records. The visit of the bank examiner does not disturb the bank whose affairs are in order.

This review by itself, however, is not enough. By auditing the quality of the records and not the quality of patient care the JCAH leaves some very large loopholes. In 1970, the commission gave only provisional accreditation to New York's Mount Sinai Hospital, generally conceded to be one of the country's finest, because of flaws in its record keeping. How many hospitals have the high quality professional staff that Mount Sinai has? Which is more important? The professional work on which a patient's survival may depend or the paperwork on which the JCAH insists? For the JCAH to give only provisional accreditation to Mount Sinai, while fully accrediting as hospitals some of the Mickey Mouse institutions with which I am familiar, is analogous to the Louvre in Paris throwing out the Mona Lisa and replacing it with one of my own artistic efforts.

There is no doubt that, in general, accredited hospitals are superior to nonaccredited ones, but there is also no doubt that an accredited hospital is not necessarily all that it should be. Some hospitals go to considerable lengths to deceive the JCAH surveyors. In one instance a hospital asked its doctors to lend their personal medical books during the period of a survey to pad out its meager library. In another, a record librarian, not wanting to be caught with a large number of incomplete records, removed them from the files and was caught hiding them in the trunk of her car. Dr. Otto Arndal, head of the JCAH accreditation program, nabbed one hospital where the minutes of meetings were so perfect that he became suspicious and nosed around a bit. Sure enough, the minutes had been made up out of whole cloth. The meetings had never been held.

These are only instances in which the Joint Commission has caught the offenders. How much deception escapes detection? As a young surgeon years ago, I assisted an older GP who was skillfully removing a hot appendix. I noticed the anaesthetist filling out a form on the patient's chart certifying that there had been a consultation prior to the operation. Later, as we redressed in the doctor's lounge, I asked the surgeon about it. He said the hospital was on only provisional accreditation because there had not been enough consultations. Consequently the anaestheist was checking every record and writing up a consultation report whenever one was lacking. The Joint Commission's diligence was rewarded the following year by a 100 percent consultation rate.

Peer review is of no value without a medical staff dedicated to making it work. All too often, especially in smaller hospitals, strong social and economic ties among the doctors insure its ineffectiveness. I served on a surgical committee some years ago that was reviewing the work of a staff surgeon whose patient records showed clearly that he was "over the hill." I suggested that we take away his operative privileges but was outvoted by those who reasoned, "Aw, Bill is a nice guy and he's got eight kids." I resigned from the committee the next day and never served again. In a recent article in *Medical Economics*, an embittered doctor reported a like experience. A surgeon at his hospital was performing many unnecessary mastoidectomies, but neither the medical staff nor the hospital administration was willing to do anything about it. The ethical physician then reported the matter to the JCAH, which was about to survey the hospital. He says the Joint Commission ignored his complaint.

At a hospital in California, trained surgeons tried to keep out of the operating room men whom they deemed unqualified. Their efforts boomeranged. The untrained men gained control of the hospital governing board, threw the trained men off the key committees, and set up their own peer review body. The JCAH, informed of what was happening, remained blissfully unconcerned as its survey team wallowed in a sea of charts. The hospital retained its accreditation. After all, the records were in good order!

Let me give yet another example of how peer review can work in actual practice. In the course of examining a young woman, I questioned her about an abdominal scar. "Oh," she said, "I had my uterus suspended when I was 18." My ears pricked up; that is a most extraordinary operation for an 18-year-old. "I was about to be married and my mother sent me to our family doctor for some premarital advice," she continued. "He checked me over and found that my uterus was tipped backward. He said I wouldn't be able to get pregnant unless it was fixed, so I had the operation two months before my wedding."

The story had a happy ending. The patient was happy when she gave birth to a healthy baby girl. The doctor was happy with his surgical triumph. His chart work was neat and so the peer review committee and the JCAH were happy. His fee was within the bounds of the "usual and customary," so the insurance carrier was happy to pay it.

But the fact is that the patient had been victimized by a physician who was flagrantly incompetent or dishonest, or both. The operation that had endangered her life was *totally unnecessary*. She would have gotten pregnant just as readily without it, and the outcome is not always so benign in such cases of "absurd surgery," as Dr. Elmer Hess, a onetime AMA president, called the performance of unnecessary uterine suspensions.

The Joint Commission is now attempting to make hospitals draw up a detailed list of exactly which procedures any given doctor may perform. On paper this sounds as though it would keep a man from getting in over his head. In practice the rule fails for the same old reason: its value depends upon the degree of peer enforcement. Dr. X hands in a list of operations he says he is capable of performing; if the medical staff accepts that list, the JCAH is satisfied, even though the doctor may in fact be unqualified to perform many or all the operations he mentions.

There are many instances where doctors who are affiliated with more than one hospital are not permitted to perform certain operations at Hospital A but are allowed to do so at Hospital B. I have known of cases where doctors have transferred patients by ambulance from A to B for that sole reason. Would TWA hire a pilot who is not good enough for United? Yet the Joint Commission has no hesitation about accrediting the B hospitals. Is the patient not entitled to as much protection when he passes through the admitting room of a hospital as he is when he passes a ticket taker at the airport?

Yet in such cases, the doctor smoothly covers himself

with the patient: "When we brought you into Hospital A, we thought it was a medical case, but now the workup shows you need an operation. I usually operate at Hospital B because my team is there; they know the instruments I like and so on. Besides, the anaesthetist is better." The patient is pleased indeed that his doctor is so concerned about his welfare, when the truth is that Hospital A thinks the doctor is incompetent and will not let him perform the operation there.

In very small hospitals, judge, jury, and plaintiff are often one and the same. An untrained surgeon may be the chairman of the committee that reviews his own work. Woe to the member who questions any operation performed by the chairman. In proprietary hospitals the chief surgeon may be the owner or one of a group of owners. Can anyone really believe that such a man will be effectively questioned by others in the hospital?

Some pathologists "play ball" with surgeons and are kind to them in their tissue reports. They may write the reports in such a way as to make a poor surgeon look good or to becloud the fact that an operation was unnecessary. What is a tissue committee to make of this gem of a pathological diagnosis: "incipient acute appendicitis, minimal, secondary to lymphoid hyperplasia with appendiclausis" (translation: normal appendix)?

Another area in which peer review has failed is that of fee splitting. In 1918, when it established its hospital standardization program, the American College of Surgeons laid down as a cardinal principle that fee splitting was to be eliminated. Yet in 1968 a headline in the ACS Newsletter read, "Regents endorse 8-point Program Against Fee Splitting." It would be hard to find a more open admission that the practice continues to flourish *half a century later*. Most appropriately, the newsletter comes from ACS headquarters in Chicago, a city notorious in the profession as a place where no young surgeon can enter practice unless he is prepared to kick back to the doctors who will send him patients.

(An ironic aspect of fee splitting is that Federal income tax law encourages it. Even where the practice is a criminal offense, as it is in some states, the splitter may deduct his kickback payments on his Federal tax return as a legitimate business expense. Under present law the Internal Revenue Service is prohibited from disallowing the deduction unless the doctor has been successfully prosecuted. To strike a body blow at fee splitting, the law should be changed to make all such payments nondeductible.)

For all the failures of peer review, the medical profession has touted it so loudly and so often that even outsiders who should know better have been taken in. The 1967 National Advisory Commission on Health Care, for example, praised the California Blue Shield plan for its excellent peer review, evidently laboring under the misconception that Blue Shield's computers control the quality of medical care. In fact the plan does nothing of the kind. What it does do is to have its computers single out unusual patterns of payment. The purpose of this is economic, to avoid making improper payments to doctors, and the medical benefits are a by-product.

The system is capable, however, of monitoring medical care quality. For example, the computers may print out the records of a doctor who claims he is seeing 100 patients a day, or of another who gives injections to every patient (some doctors average *more* than one injection per patient!) In these cases two possibilities exist. The doctors may be claiming to do more work than they are in fact doing. In that case they are crooks, and Blue Shield can have them cut out of the Medicaid program, as it has done in a very few instances, or it could even prosecute. On the other hand, if the doctors are actually doing what they say they are, then they are usually charlatans because it is physically impossible for a physician to give reasonable attention to 100 patients a day and because obviously not all patients need injections. Blue Shield refers such cases to the doctors' peers—their local medical societies.

And we are back where we started. What I have said about hospital peer review applies also to review by local medical societies, especially the smaller ones. The members are friends and frequent associates; they may play golf together, and their wives may meet weekly at the bridge table. They are dependent upon one another economically for referrals. They have a normal human reluctance to go after "old Bill" even though he is clearly slipping. Nelson Cruikshank, director of the National Council of Senior Citizens, has commented upon the "natural reluctance of persons with so many economic and social interests to take punitive action against one of their number to enforce standards. This is true whether the group is a medical society, a bar association or a labor union." His assertion is borne out by a recent American Bar Association report which termed the self-policing practices of the legal profession "a scandalous situation." The report could have been written about doctors: "With few exceptions, the prevailing attitude of lawyers toward disciplinary enforcement ranges from apathy to outright hostility. Disciplinary action is practically nonexistent in many jurisdictions."

Dr. Wesley W. Hall, a surgeon who has been elected the

AMA's 1971–72 president, tells of having participated in peer review in his home town of Reno, Nevada, and making it work. But he did so, he adds with a smile, only by being "a self-propelled, rotating bastard." Unhappily for the public and the profession, there are not enough such bastards to go around. There should have been one on the review committee of one small hospital in southern California that I know of where a single unqualified surgeon performed more of one particular type of kidney operation in ten years than all the surgeons at the Mayo Clinic together have done in fifty.

In New York City the directors of the Medicaid program have undertaken some peer review. When a question arises about the practices of a doctor, he gets a telephone call. If he gives his permission, *and only if he does so*, his office is visited by another doctor, always a man in the same specialty, who goes over a sampling of his records with him and may offer suggestions for improvement. Mild though it is, this peer review has been fought bitterly by the state medical association as an intrusion of government into medical practice!

Dr. James Z. Appel, a past president of the AMA, has publicly recognized the failings of peer review by cronies. He suggested that the function be removed from county to state medical societies so that the work of a man under judgment could be reviewed by a disinterested stranger from another community instead of by his cronies in town. The AMA gave this proposal about as warm a welcome as a hairy hippie might expect at an Elks Club banquet.

I have severely indicted our health system for tolerating second-class doctors and second-class hospitals, an unholy alliance rendering second-class care to patients who are often unaware that they are second-class medical citizens. Current controls are inadequate for insuring a quality of care that the public deserves and the medical profession is capable of providing.

So medical audits and peer review are far from an unqualified success in maintaining high hospital standards. *Why don't our well-audited and peer-reviewed hospitals measure up to the performance of the hospitals in Sweden or England* where peer review is relatively uncommon? Further, is peer review all that important at such well-regulated medical centers as the Mayo Clinic, Johns Hopkins, or Massachusetts General? What will more surely lead to high quality care, measuring a doctor's output or controlling a doctor's input?

Medicine had better answer these questions. Public patience is wearing thin. At a 1970 meeting of the American Hospital Association, Senator Edward M. Kennedy proposed that hospital administrations take over from the doctors responsibility for policing the quality of medical care. It is no longer enough, he said, to send cases of misfeasance "over to the county medical society for burial."

10

SOMETHING CAN BE DONE

AT the risk of taxing the reader's patience, I repeat my axiom: the most important component of medical care quality is the competence of the physician who renders the service. With the axiom goes a corollary: we can improve the quality of care more immediately, more easily, and more substantially by restricting doctors to rendering those services they are competent to perform than by any other single step. In other words, we will be farther ahead if we get rid of what union official Melvin Glasser rightly referred to as "rotten" care than if we get overly concerned about optimal care.

We have some objective standards that help to measure the quality of care in a hospital. Committee reports on the number of normal appendixes and normal uteri removed, the rates of infection, of morbidity and of mortality, and the caesarian section rate are of obvious value in judging hospital standards. On the other hand, such statistics as the number of times doctors visit the hospital per patient and the number of laboratory tests ordered or of consultations requested are almost worthless as measures of quality. As Robert Meyers, former assistant director of the

American College of Surgeons, put it, "Hospitals are the only major business in which unreliable statistics are thoughtlessly selected, laboriously collected, promiscuously dissected and unreservedly accepted as facts which accurately gauge achievements."

Much of what is done in a hospital never shows up in statistical data. Data do not show when a man performs the wrong operation or does not operate at all when he should. They do not show that while he was skillfully removing an appendix he did not recognize a nearby cancer. Auditing hospital care measures output and, although of value, is secondary in my view; the real concern should be with input. Control over who performs what operation is of far greater importance than a statistical analysis of results after the operations have been completed and some damage has been done.

A study of the medical care received by families of teamsters union members in New York revealed some astonishing variations in quality. Only 31 percent of the general medical care was of high quality, but 100 percent of treatment for diseases of the eye was. Why the disparity? Ophthalmology, says the union's report, is "a highly specialized area, where physicians not trained in the field rarely venture to perform procedures." Exactly so!

Yet the eye is not the most important organ of the body. People almost never die from eye surgery. Many abdominal operations are more complicated and difficult—and are associated with far, far higher mortality rates—than are most eye operations. Why, then, do untrained doctors venture into the more dangerous area and not into the less dangerous one? Because only the operator and his assistants know what a doctor has actually done inside one's abdominal cavity, but everyone can see the results of eye surgery. The ophthalmologist can not easily hide his mistakes. I suspect, too, that ophthalmology is a specialty most widely recognized by the general public; almost everybody knows that if you have eye trouble you go to an eye doctor. Unfortunately not enough people recognize that other forms of surgery should also be performed by surgeons in the appropriate specialty. Only 50 percent of the 15 million operations done annually in the United States are performed by or under the supervision of board certified surgeons or members of the ACS. Incredible as it may seem, *millions* of operations are performed each year by physicians who have had no special surgical training.

The only thing that stops the Joint Commission on Accreditation of Hospitals from adopting the rule that surgery shall be performed only by qualified surgeons (a rule that applies to military and VA hospitals) is the roar of protest that would arise from the untrained doctors who would have to give up those lucrative surgical practices for which they are not qualified. In the commission's concentration on the medical environment in the past "only the narrowest edge of the substance of medical care itself has been broached," as a former JCAH official put it.

I submit that the time has come for the JCAH to reverse course and begin to judge "the substance of medical care itself." Qualified physicians in every specialty are recognized by their respective medical specialty boards. These boards are officially recognized by the AMA as representing the highest standards of medical practice. Why should not the Joint Commission adopt and apply those standards? Is it unreasonable to insist that the physician who assumes the responsibility for the patient's life on the operating table at least be trained to perform the operation? Is it revolutionary to believe that adequate training is more important than so refined and subtle a measure of quality as that "ingredient of professional judgment" that the AMA talks about?

Though there might be many a painful wrench at the start, the JCAH has the power to apply such standards. Accreditation is important to hospitals for many reasons. The power and importance of the Joint Commission was recognized by the Federal Government when the law accepted JCAH accreditation as the standard for hospitals' admitting Medicare patients. The JCAH has the power, and that power should be used.

The Federal Government also has an important role to play here. Since it foots 38 percent of our total national health bill, it has a real financial interest in discouraging unnecessary surgery and substandard, and therefore more costly, hospital care. Yet in this field, the Government wears the two faces of Janus. It has one standard for VA and military patients, another for those on Medicare and Medicaid. The military standards are indeed high. Presidents and congressmen know this well: when they themselves are sick, they go to the Walter Reed Army Hospital or the Bethesda Naval Hospital. People under the HEW programs do not have that privilege.

Certainly the Medicare and Medicaid arms of HEW should be as concerned about the dangers to the patient of an untrained surgeon as another branch of the department, the Food and Drug Administration, is about dangerous drugs. Perhaps the FDA takes its cue from Shylock's impassioned outburst in *The Merchant of Venice*: "If you poison us, do we not die?" HEW might remember that he also said, "If you prick us, do we not bleed?"

The Government could give an enormous and immeddiate lift to the quality of medical care simply by limiting payment for procedures performed under Medicare and Medicaid to doctors qualified to do those procedures. The cost saving would also be impressive. I suspect that the ripples made by casting such a stone into the water would spread far beyond the immediate splash. The Blue Cross programs and health insurance companies who act as fiscal intermediaries for Medicare and Medicaid inevitably would see the advantages of extending the rule to the people whom they cover privately.

I am well aware of the outcry these proposals will raise from a segment of the medical profession. It will be said that the regulation of surgery, like all regulation, deprives the individual of freedom of choice. In fact, the only freedom the patient would lose is the right to let some unqualified man take chances with his life. Some doctors would lose the right to take those chances, and well they should.

Are Americans less free because stockbrokers are restrained from selling watered stocks? Are we less free because shady real estate agents are prevented from selling lots that can be seen only when the tide is out? Dr. Milton Roemer, professor of public health at the University of California at Los Angeles, asks, "Is the veteran served by a surgeon in a government hospital less free because the VA requires that the doctor be board-certified to do the operation?"

Private hospitals should not be pure examples of free enterprise. In 1909 the Carnegie Foundation made the following statement in supporting the Flexner report: "The attitude of the Foundation is that all colleges and universities [substitute "all hospitals"], whether supported by taxation or private endowment, are in truth public service corporations, and that the public is entitled to know the facts concerning their administration and development. . . ." Sixty years later this AMA-endorsed statement reflects the contemporary philosophy of hospital service: "Hospitals, regardless of size or type, must provide proper safeguards for the public." Wilbur Cohen, former Secretary of HEW, expressed the prevailing feeling of many health authorities concerned with the quality of hospital practice: "Are we coming to a point where health care facilities may have to be looked upon as a public utility subject to the kind of public policy constraints exercised over public utilities?"

While regulation should start in the hospital, controls are needed over office practices too. Though private office care is far harder to monitor than the more visible hospital care, there are gangrenous practices that need to be amputated. For example, there are doctors without a day's training in x-ray diagnosis who install low powered equipment in their offices and decide such important questions as whether a patient has stomach cancer or a diseased gallbladder on the basis of amateurish radiological studies. They collect the same fees from health insurers of Medicare and Medicaid as would a board-certified radiologist who has performed a highly sophisticated examination. Is it really too much to ask that a doctor who reads x-ray films be required to learn how to interpret them so that his patients are maximally protected from a missed diagnosis? Here again, if the Federal Government were to set up standards for Medicare and Medicaid patients, there would be a substantial cost saving, and the general level of quality would rise as health insurers adopted the same standards for their own policyholders.

The Federal Government could also use its health insurance programs as a stick to prod the fiscal intermediaries to adopt and refine the California Blue Shield system of checking on office practices by computer. An analysis of charges for vitamin B_{12} injections, for example, might show that the patients of one doctor suffer from pernicious anemia 100 times more frequently than do the patients of the doctor down the street. The doctor who treats his fracture patients by giving them infrared treatment through a cast (which the rays will not penetrate) to "promote bone healing" might well be visited by one of his peers, as now sometimes happens under New York City's Medicaid program. I could give many more examples of poor office practices, but these will do for a start.

After we have corrected the most easily correctable substandard medical care—bad practices by the incompetent—the next step follows logically. A well-qualified technically competent specialist who engages in dubious medical practices should be condemned even more than the untrained doctor who strays outside his area of expertise. Kidneys are being well suspended, but should not have been suspended in the first place. Carotid bodies are being beautifully removed from the neck, but why? There are plenty of other examples of the well-performed operation that should not have been performed at all. And then there are those brilliantly executed operations performed under ethical clouds—ghost surgery and fee splitting. There is room for upgrading of care among specialists as well as nonspecialists.

I suggest that we approach the problem of raising the quality of medical care as though it were a pyramid. Let us begin by slicing off the broad layer of rot at the bottom and then refine our way upward from there. For example, following the precedent set by the American Board of Family Practice, I believe the other specialty boards will soon begin to make specialists take periodic new examinations, so that a man once qualified will have to keep up and stay qualified to keep his certification. I am all for this kind of refinement, but higher on my list of priorities than making the best even better is getting rid of the worst. That will most quickly and efficiently raise the level of care. Let us improve the quality of care at all levels, but let us begin by seeing to it that the present well-established standards of excellence are universally adhered to. Every patient is entitled to a competent doctor.

11

"YOU GET WHAT YOU PAY FOR"—
OR DO YOU?

EVERYBODY knows that you get what you pay for; you cannot expect all the features and quality of a Cadillac for a Chevrolet price. So high quality medical care has to cost more than low quality care. Right? Let's see.

A 40-year-old man hurt his back and was admitted to the hospital (it was accredited) for diagnosis and treatment. X-ray studies showed that he had fractured his spine. His gallbladder and stomach were also x-rayed, and both these organs were shown to be perfectly normal. His doctor did not treat the spine injury; instead he removed the healthy gallbladder. The pathologist's report confirmed the x-ray finding of a normal gallbladder. Unfortunately the surgical incision broke down, and the patient required yet another operation to repair the hernia before he could go back to work.

The man's hospital and doctor bills for both operations came to some $3000. His lost time from work came to a like amount. The public made up part of that $6000 by paying him unemployment insurance. The Prudential Insurance Company cheerfully paid the major portion of the medical bill, which it deemed "reasonable." In the end, of course, their policyholders paid for it in their premiums, adding a little extra for the company's stockholders. Prudential could not care less that the operation was ghosted and that the patient never met his surgeon either before or after the operation. The company probably never even knew that no operative report was entered in the chart.

If he had been cared for by a better doctor in the first place, this patient would have been fitted with a back brace. He would have stayed out of the hospital altogether and would have lost relatively little time from work. A higher quality medical care would not only have avoided needless pain and risk to life, but would have cost far, far less than the care he did receive.

I know of no way to estimate how many of our health-care dollars are flushed needlessly down the drain in this way, but the total must be staggering. Surely this case and others I have cited provide a clue to the problem of containing health-care costs. It hardly needs to be said that these costs must be contained. The rise will continue inexorably, but we must keep it to the minimum.

Doctors are acutely aware of the factors that are driving up health-care costs. Most of us make every effort to spare the patient's pocketbook. Our professional organizations are actively cooperating with numerous plans and programs to contain costs. Naturally, then, doctors are disturbed by irresponsible reports that put medicine falsely in an unfavorable light.

Let us take a single example: a published report showed that a Kentucky country doctor got $81,726.63 from Medicaid in 1968 and $106,112.06 in 1969. The report is true. That fellow must be one terrible gouger, mustn't he? Imagine the life he leads with all that money, lolling on his yacht, taking showers in champagne, and whooping it up in the fleshpots!

The doctor in question, Paul F. Maddox of Campton, wrote an article for *American Medical News* telling exactly what he did to get that money and what he did with it. To begin with, he serves one of the poorest areas in the United States: 52.8 percent of the local families are below the official poverty level. There is no other doctor nearby. The nearest hospital bed is 45 miles away.

Dr. Maddox has office hours from 8 A.M. until 9 P.M., 365 days a year. On Thanksgiving Day in 1969 he saw 117 patients. He maintains a 24-hour call service, sees every sick person who walks in his door, and seldom gets to bed before 2 A.M. In 1969 he saw 49,209 patients, an average of 135.8 a day, and delivered 399 babies. To help him do all this, he employed thirteen nursing assistants and, on a part-time basis, eleven moonlighting residents of a university hospital. His overhead costs in 1968 were $123,471.62 and in 1969 were $150,000. The money goes about one-third for salaries, one-third for drugs and supplies, and one-third for all other costs.

Dr. Maddox charged $70 for delivering a baby, and this included an eight-hour bed stay in his clinic. This, as he freely agrees, is far from the ideal way to have a baby, but it is an improvement over having one at home with no attendance at all, and it saves the state at least $230 compared to the cost of delivery at the university hospital, assuming the patient could get there, which she usually cannot. At Dr. Maddox's 400-a-year delivery rate, that item alone amounts to a public saving of $92,000. More than half of Dr. Maddox's patients are eligible for neither Medicaid or Medicare, though many of them are so poor that they can pay little or nothing. He delivered five babies for one woman who was able to pay him only $25 for all five. He has more than $200,000 on his account books which, he said, "I hope to collect after the Resurrection."

Some yacht! Some fleshpots!

Some doctors *are* gougers. Some *are* getting rich. Most doctors earn incomes well above the average. But the number of gougers and of those who will become millionaires is small indeed. Most doctors, especially those in solo practice, earn their incomes by working hard. For them the 60-hour work week is average, and even the 70-hour work week is not uncommon. It has frequently been said that a union plumber or electrician would earn more than the average doctor does if he worked as long hours.

Doctors' fees have been climbing, 37.1 percent from 1960 to 1968 while the general cost of living rose 17.5 percent. During this same period, hospital costs rose 101.1 percent, and that item is by far the largest component of health-care cost. Doctors get $.20 of the health-care dollar, hospitals $.38.

Hospital costs not only will not come down, but will undoubtedly continue to go up. The single most important element in hospital cost is wages, about two-thirds of the average institution's expense being payroll. Until very recently the hospital worker was cruelly exploited. Hours were brutally long, with many jobs being covered for 24 hours by two people working 12-hour shifts. Pay was unbelievably low. In 1946—when a hospital bed cost $9.50 a day—the average hospital employee's wage was $1226 a year, while her sister in the factory across town was earning more than three times as much, $3900. As recently as

1963, some hospitals paid ironers and kitchen helpers less than $.50 an hour. Nurses have long earned less than garbage collectors.

Hospital employees are no longer willing to be "captive philanthropists," subsidizing the institution by accepting substandard pay. Federal minimum wage laws now apply to hospitals. Workers are unionizing, demanding and getting better pay. But it costs! A 1970 wage settlement by San Francisco hospitals added from $11 to $15 a day to room costs. Despite such whopping increases, hospital employees still have not caught up with people doing comparable work in other industries, with the lag being as great as 25 percent in some places. Hospital costs will soar in the next few years as that lag is made up.

Not only do hospitals have to pay their people more, but they need more of them. With shorter work weeks, it now takes five workers to cover a given job 24 hours a day, seven days a week, where formerly three workers were sufficient. The miracles of modern medicine also require more employees. Back in those happy $9.50-a-day times of 1946, no hospital had costly heart-lung equipment or teams of highly skilled, highly paid technicians to operate it. Those things did not exist. Today they are saving thousands of lives every year, but they do not come cheap. Just maintaining a kidney dialysis unit, for example, costs $60,000 a year. As a result of all this, the number of hospital employees per 100 patients has grown from 156 in 1946 to 279 today. A large hospital in 1971 may have more than 200 job classifications.

But per diem cost is not everything. Consider, for example, that before the discovery of antibiotics a pneumonia patient might have paid as little as $5 a day for his bed, but he invariably had a stormy course. Frequently he developed such complications as empyema, which required several chest operations. At best he usually spent weeks, even months, in the hospital, losing earning time from his work. At worst he died, and that happened frequently. In New York's Bellevue Hospital in those days, the staff called pneumonia "the old man's friend." When a patient over the age of 65 was admitted with pneumonia, the admitting doctor automatically made out and signed the death certificate, leaving to be filled in only the time when the inevitable would happen! Today a pneumonia patient usually leaves his high cost bed within a week—cured.

Which really cost more, the poor quality cheap care of the old days or the high quality care of today? By the time you add up the cost of many days in the hospital, many doctor visits, and earnings loss of the old days, it is quite probable that they will total up to a *higher* dollar cost than modern care. And what price do you put on the suffering alleviated and the lives saved?

What really matters is not the cost per day, but the total cost of the illness, which leads us to another seeming paradox in this curious intertwinement of quality and cost. It is an axiom that the sooner a doctor can send a patient home from the hospital, without undue risk, the better for all concerned. Patients usually thrive better at home; they go back to work earlier and the hospital frees a bed for someone else. Yet the short stay is more costly per day. That is because a patient uses most of the hospital's costly ancillary services at the beginning of his stay. That is when he uses the operating room, x-ray equipment, and labs, and when he requires intensive nursing care. Later on as he recovers, he uses far fewer of these services. On a long stay, these costs average out over many days; on a short one, they can be averaged only over fewer days and thus raise the cost per day. Thus an efficient short-stay hospital has a higher per diem rate than an inefficient one, but the cost to the patient is generally lower. A seven-day stay at $75 costs $525; a five-day stay at $85 is $100 less!

It has been my experience that medical consumers, whether they be individual patients or the managers of union health plans, are less concerned about the cost of medical service per se than they are about two other matters: the quality of that service and their ability to budget the cost with reasonable accuracy and thus avoid the icy shock of a huge and unexpected bill. I have also found that dissatisfaction with the bill seems to exist in direct ratio to dissatisfaction with the results. The patient who feels that he has had good care seldom expresses unhappiness with the bill, though he may be extremely dissatisfied with the extent of his insurance coverage. When he believes that he has not received good medical attention, however, the patient may well say, "Why should I spend all this money when I didn't get well?" And he may well say that even if his insurance covers the whole bill. No matter how low the fee may be, if he thinks he has been shortchanged in his care, the patient feels that it has been money wasted.

Of course, I deplore exorbitant fees. As I have said, there are gougers among us, and they are difficult to control when there is so severe a shortage of physicians. Many of them will be forced into line by economic checks when we have enough doctors, but even then some will still require the whip of strict controls. The greedy have always been with us. In the fourth century B.C., the physicians of Rome were admonished, "Where there is a question of fee, the medical officer must take as a standard, not what men fearing death will agree to pay, but what men recovering from illness will offer."

My own experience in the matter of patients' attitudes toward fees is borne out by a survey of 3000 families undertaken in 1970 for *Medical Economics*. The magazine found that 76 percent thought the family doctor deserves just about what he earns, while 15 percent thought he ought to earn more. Some 73 percent thought the family doctor's fees were about right, and another 5 percent thought they were too low. As to surgeons, 65 percent thought fees were about right or too low, while for medical specialists the figure was 60 percent. Some 58 percent of the patients said their family doctors has raised fees in recent years. Of these, 50 percent were "very well satisfied" with the physicians' explanations, and another 38 percent were "fairly well satisfied."

None of the foregoing is meant to say that medical costs can be allowed to rise unchecked. For people on fixed incomes, medical care costs, like other forms of inflation, can be a severe hardship. The aged, whose incomes are stagnant and whose medical costs are heavy, have found some relief in Medicare, though it still covers only about 45 percent of their costs. The doctor cannot wash his hands of the cost problem. He is responsible for much more of the medical care dollar than the $.20 he himself collects. One has little choice but to buy the drugs he prescribes. He admits the patient to the hospital, controls what is done to him there, and discharges him. Directly or indirectly he is answerable for fully 80 percent of private health-care outlays.

Hence organized medicine, together with other private groups and government, is searching for ways to keep down costs. Many approaches have been suggested by the various parties. Two of these are the encouragement of group practice and the widespread use of physicians' assistants, which I have dealt with in detail in Chapters 5 and 6, but I will say here that I can not see either as offering any vast monetary savings. For the time being, let us look at some of the other proposals.

One of these is to make greater use of generic drugs, as opposed to those with brand names. The Federal Government unquestionably saves worthwhile sums by buying generics for its hospitals. A sizable private hospital that can exert strict quality controls can also save some money this way, and many of them do. Some patients, such as arthritics and diabetics, need to take maintenance drugs for long periods of time, even for life, and it can be very important indeed to such people to get the cheapest acceptable version of the drug. But generic prescribing is not a cure-all, any more than is the drug being prescribed. For one thing, many of the drugs we use are taken only once or on rare occasions, such as antibiotics that are discontinued when the infection has cleared up. In these instances the savings to the patient may be small. For another thing, prices even of generics may fluctuate wildly. Consumers Union recently sent shoppers to 60 drugstores in the New York metropolitan area to buy 30 capsules of tetracycline, a standard antibiotic. The prices they paid ranged from $.79 to $7.45, almost ten times as high! Even two branches of the same chain charged different prices, in one case $.79, in the other $3.65. Consumers Union's experience suggests that, while prescribing generics may save money, careful shopping can save even more.

Another proposal is that Government set fee schedules, flat amounts that doctors may charge Medicaid patients for specified services. I seriously doubt that this can be effective. The type doctor who extracts unconscionable fees cannot be trusted to observe a fee schedule, and he can easily get around it. To such a man every cold becomes pneumonia and every wart is a skin cancer; no patient leaves his office without the benefit of a shot. The integrity of the physician is of far more importance than a fee schedule in holding the line on prices.

Another proposal that is being touted as a big cost saver is the provision of more out-of-hospital medical benefits which, it is argued, will cut down on the necessity for in-hospital care. In 1969 Blue Cross and Blue Shield tried an eight-month experiment in Wichita, Kansas, by extending a wide range of such benefits to 13,000 persons at no extra charge. Nonsurgical admissions and days of stay did decrease by about one-fifth for stays of ten or fewer days. But for stays of ten days and longer, such admissions and days increased by more than 10 percent. The extension of benefits had had a two-fold impact: admissions for minor illnesses were cut down because satisfactory nonhospital treatment could be had, but the availability of diagnostic services encouraged people to use them and so illnesses were turned up that otherwise would have gone untreated. Those illnesses were chronic and serious, requiring long stays. It was certainly a good thing to keep out of the hospital people who did not really need to be there and to get into the hospital those who did, but it did not save any money.

Nor do I believe that comprehensive health planning will keep medical bills down by very much. The basic idea here is to avoid duplication within a given region of expensive hospital facilities. If Hospitals A and B both have emergency rooms and obstetrical wards, and if these facilities are only half used, why not have A close its obstetrical ward and send all the babies to be born over to B, while B shuts down its emergency room and all the trauma cases go to A? This kind of thing has been done in some places and to good effect, since a facility that is kept busy usually offers better care than one that is seldom used. But, again, the monetary saving has been relatively small.

Regional health planners are also studying their areas to find out what new facilities may be needed and to encourage their development. All to the good. They are also trying to discourage the development of any facilities that they see as duplicating ones already in existence. On this point, Dr. Ben Chaiken, executive director of the Arizona Tuberculosis and Health Association, said, "Not duplicating expensive specialized services will eliminate some costs to institutions enlarging their facilities or to new institutions. However, the 'savings' to the consumer of medical care will be infinitesimal. The issue of not duplicating specialized services borders on the irrelevant." I agree.

There is also the human problem. A community hospital installs a $75,000 x-ray unit in a surgical suite for use in certain neurosurgical operations. The equipment is used less than ten hours a month, and similar machines exist at other hospitals not too far away. Let us look at a specific case. An internist, after a lengthy workup, diagnoses a patient as having a brain tumor. A neurologist confirms the diagnosis. The patient needs an operation requiring that x-ray equipment. Should we now transfer him to another hospital? He and his family would be unhappy about the inconvenience of moving outside their community, the internist would be unhappy because he could not follow his patient, and the neurosurgeon's reaction need not be described. Sheer mechanical efficiency might dictate the transfer, but neither the practioners of medicine nor their patients are machines. As Dr. Anne Somers of Princeton University has said, "I am afraid that improved hospital management has been oversold as an answer to the costs problem. It is no panacea: there is simply not that much waste to be squeezed out of the operating budget of most hospitals nor that many additional dollars to be squeezed out of the patients being treated."

Finally, no conference on health-care financing would be complete without some expert explaining how we can lower costs by greater emphasis on preventive medicine, and automated multiphasic screening (AMS) is urged as the way to go about it. From the patient's viewpoint, AMS is much like an army induction examination. You travel along a medical assembly line with a technician here drawing blood and collecting urine, one there x-raying your chest, and so on. Test results and other data are then fed into a computer which prints out a record for the doctor, flagging anything unusual enough to deserve his special attention. AMS centers are springing up about the countryside like dandelions and are supposed to be able to discover what ails you before you know anything does. In theory the doctor can then head off trouble at its beginning.

The trouble is that nobody knows whether this works or not or, if so, at what cost. The Kaiser Foundation has been offering AMS to its subscribers at great expense since 1964 and is now in the midst of a ten-year study of its value. They are checking 45,000 people who regularly receive AMS examinations against a control group and at mid-point in the study concede that they cannot yet show that one group is any healthier than the other. Some tests were discontinued because they were found to be not worth-while. Others were found by the Kaiser people to be highly useful, among them mammography in postmeno-pausal women, an x-ray test that shows up tumors of the breast too small to be felt. Until the Kaiser study and simi-lar studies being conducted under the auspices of HEW are completed, we simply will not know the overall value of AMS or of most of its component parts. We should not expect too much or we will be disappointed. What can a computerized examination detect that would prevent or change the course of a coronary thrombosis, cancer, stroke, or arthritis? Thus far we do know that the uses of automa-tion for patient care can be expensive. At Boston's Peter Bent Brigham Hospital, the installation of an automated hospital-outpatient system upped the cost of each patient visit about one dollar.

The plain truth is that we can reduce the costs of medi-cal care by preventing disease far more in our homes and in our daily lives than we can in the doctor's office. Cutting out cigarettes will do far more to stop lung cancer, with all its attendant human and financial costs, than anything that the doctors can do. Moderating our use of alcohol would drastically improve our health and save millions. So would fluoridating all our drinking water. If we could wipe out all cancer, we would add two or three years to life expectancy in this country, but if all our obese citizens were to reduce to ideal weight, it has been estimated that we would add more than double that—about seven years. The annual physical examination may be all very well, particularly if you are a company executive or a union member who gets it free (meaning that the public pays for it in higher prices), but essentially preventive medicine for adults is a do-it-yourself thing—a change in eating, drinking, smoking, and drive-to-work habits.

In the doctor's office, as in the hospital, quality and cost cannot be divorced from each other, though one must never make the mistake of thinking that medical efficiency is like efficiency on an automobile production line. Ten years ago, like most surgeons, I treated women with cysts of the breast by operating upon them in the hospital under general anaesthesia. The two-day stay plus surgeon's and anaesthetist's fees generally added up to about $250. Then new medical knowledge caused many of us to change our method of treatment. Now we remove the fluid from such cysts in the office under local anaesthesia and with equally good results. The office charge may be $15 to $25, a saving of at least $225 per patient. There is no way of knowing how many thousands and thousands of dollars my colleagues have saved for many, many women in this way in the past ten years. In addition these women lost no time from work, paid for no baby sitters, and suffered none of the inconveniences of hospitalization. We surgeons believe that this more efficient technique is worth at least as much to the patient as are power brakes on her new automobile. But she does not even know about it!

I have cited many other examples from my own experience of how quality care costs less, but let us look at a more general picture.

Tonsillectomies are performed under California's Medicaid program at the rate of 40 per 1000 children under sixteen. I am familiar with fee-for-service group practice clinics where the rate is only 3.9 per 1000 children—less than one-tenth the Medicaid rate. The annual cost of systematically relieving California's indigent children of their tonsils is $6 million. At least $5 million of that sum could be saved if California surgery were properly regulated. This saving would come from controlling just one relatively inexpensive operation in just one state!

Several studies show the savings to be made when surgery is restricted to qualified doctors. When the United Mine Workers ruled some years ago that thereafter surgery in their hospitals was to be performed only by board-certified men, the surgery rate was cut in half. One of the most interesting studies is of Federal Government employees, who are offered their choice of any of several health benefit plans. Those who elect Blue Shield coverage, of course, choose their own doctors, who may or may not be qualified specialists. Those who choose the big prepaid group plans, like Kaiser or the Health Insurance Plan of Greater New York, are assured that only qualified men will be allowed to operate on them. In 1966 the surgery rate for those who chose group practice plans was 31 per 1000 persons. For the Blue Shield group, it was more than double that, 73 per 1000. Consider the rate for four operations most often done needlessly: gallbladder, 1.4 per 1000 for the group practice patients, 1.9 for Blue Shield; appendectomy, 1.1 versus 2.2; "female surgery," 4.5 versus 8.8; and tonsillectomy, 1.9 versus 8.4!

Studies of medical practices where quality is rigidly controlled indicate that $2.5 billion could be saved nationally in hospital costs alone if such controls were universal. Very nearly as much more could then certainly be saved in physician fees and prescription costs. Moreover, quality controls would greatly ameliorate, if not altogether eliminate, hospital bed and nursing shortages. The Kaiser hospitals require only 59 percent as many beds per person as does the state of California generally, and three quarters of this saving in beds is the direct result of lower admission rates. Similarly, Kaiser's per person cost for providing hospital care is only 61 percent of the state's average cost. While there are other factors at play in the Kaiser system, the primary reason for its economy is that *due to rigid quality controls, doctors do not hospitalize patients needlessly.* I do not say that the Kaiser plan should be applied to everybody (in fact, I believe that it has some serious shortcomings). But I do say that quality controls as rigid as Kaiser's should be universally applied. Is there any other single step that would have such far-reaching, salutary effects on medical care quality and costs?

12

IS NATIONAL HEALTH INSURANCE
THE ANSWER?

JACK and Bill both worked for the same painting contractor. One day at 4:45 P.M., just before quitting time, Jack was painting the outside walls of a medical office building when his scaffolding slipped. He plunged 30 feet to the ground and suffered compound fractures of both legs.

That day Bill was working on another job. He knocked off at 5 P.M. and started home. At 5:15 a drunk ran a red light and slammed into his car. Bill, too, suffered compound fractures of both legs.

The two men arrived at the same hospital within a few minutes of each other. After treatment they were given adjoining beds. Each remained in the hospital for six weeks. Each spent another six months at home before he returned to work, fully recovered.

Similar cases? There is one major difference between the two—that little matter of the 5 o'clock whistle. Jack was hurt on the job; Bill was injured on his own time. Their employer was required by law to carry workman's compensation insurance, so Jack's doctor and hospital bills were completely paid. He also got a weekly check as partial compensation for lost wages, so his family did not suffer financial hardship. That insurance coverage stopped at quitting time and did not apply to Bill's accident. For some reason, any reason, he had no insurance of his own. His injury was a financial disaster. His savings were wiped out, he ran into debt, his wife had to find a job, and a long-anticipated vacation trip had to be canceled.

Society provides compulsory health insurance for the breadwinner who is injured on the job, but not for him after working hours. Why not? What is there about a 5 o'clock whistle that determines whether or not a person is covered?

Patients are concerned not only about the quality and price of medical care, but about how to pay for it. A serious disease or accident can be a financial catastrophe, even for people with quite sizable incomes. The only possible answer is prepaid health insurance that spreads the risk over the largest possible group. The idea is universally accepted now, but it was not always so.

Health insurance in the United States began in 1778 when Congress established the Marine Hospital Service (now the Public Health Service). From each seaman's wage, there was a compulsory deduction of $.20 a month, for which he was entitled to free hospital and medical care, such as it was in those days. Private health insurance started half a century later when several companies were organized to provide coverage against railroad and steamboat accidents, much like the travel policies sold at airport counters and vending machines today. The business grew, and by 1900 there were 47 companies offering accident insurance.

A major breakthrough came in 1929 when a group of

schoolteachers in Dallas, Texas, arranged with Baylor University to give them hospital care on a prepaid basis; this was the origin of Blue Cross. The movement spread rapidly during the Depression when hospitals, desperate because people could not pay their bills, embraced it as a means of financial salvation. World War II added tremendous impetus. Because wage increases were severely limited by law, labor unions sought other benefits for their members, and health coverage—paid for in part or in whole by employers—came to be widely written into contracts. Today more than 80 percent of the U.S. population has some form of health insurance, although in all too many, if not most, cases, it is sorely inadequate.

The AMA has waxed hot and cold on health insurance. During its Golden Age early in this century, Dr. Alexander Lambert, chairman of its Social Insurance Committee and personal physician to Theodore Roosevelt, strongly advocated a state-administered compulsory health insurance system. Largely under his prodding, the AMA Board of Trustees resolved in 1916: "The time has come when we can no longer resist the social movement. It is better that we initiate the necessary changes than have them forced upon us." The following year the AMA adopted a resolution stating, "The profession should earnestly study to solve the questions of medical care that will arise under various forms of social insurance. Blind opposition, indignant repudiation, bitter denunciation of these laws is worse than useless; it leads nowhere and it leaves the profession in a position of helplessness as the rising tide of social development sweeps over it." How prophetic!

During and immediately after World War I, the character of the AMA's leadership changed completely and "blind opposition, indignant repudiation" became the rule. During the Depression President Hoover appointed a Committee on the Costs of Medical Care headed by Dr. Ray Lyman Wilbur, his secretary of the Interior and a past president of the AMA. The majority report of the committee recommended "that medical service . . . be largely furnished by groups of physicians . . . [and] that the costs of medical care be placed on a group payment basis through the use of taxation or through the use of both of these methods."

The AMA's repudiation reached new heights of indignation: voluntary insurance was "socialism and communism . . . inciting to a revolution." Group practices were "medical Soviets." Said the *Journal* of the AMA under the editorship of Dr. Morris Fishbein, "Voluntary insurance schemes are now in operation in many parts of the United States. . . . Wherever they are established there is solicitation of patients, destructive competition among professional groups, inferior medical service, loss of personal relationship of patient and physician and demoralization of the profession." On another occasion organized medicine found that for doctors "to traffic in financial protection against the day of illness . . . savors of the commercial and smacks of the socialistic." (Such bitter words must have stung deeply. Almost forty years later in 1970, Dr. Fishbein, long gone from the AMA, introduced as a luncheon speaker Dr. Richard L. Wilbur, now assistant executive vice president of that organization. Dr. Wilbur began his talk by saying he was glad to have so generous an introduction "from a man who called my grandfather a Communist.")

In 1933 the AMA attacked Blue Cross and rebuked the

ACS for endorsing it: "No third party must be permitted to come between the patient and his physician in any medical relation." In 1938 the AMA's blind opposition to prepaid group practice landed it in court. The national organization and the Medical Society of the District of Columbia were indicted under the Sherman Anti-Trust Act for restraining the practice of medicine, and the AMA was fined $2500.

Eventually, pocketbook interest overcame even the granite prejudices of the AMA leadership. Hospitals were obviously pleased with Blue Cross because it was paying bills they might otherwise never collect. Blue Shield was established to perform a like service for the doctor. By 1949 the AMA was endorsing private health insurance as the "American way." Its opposition to Government-sponsored health insurance remained unchanged, however, as it demonstrated by the bitterness and costliness of its losing fight against Medicare. By 1969 the organization had come full circle on private insurance. Its president, Dr. Dwight L. Wilbur, son of Dr. Ray Lyman Wilbur and uncle of Dr. Richard, urged doctors "to help make the people of this country aware that it is to their distinct benefit to pay in advance for health care."

We have at last arrived at a national consensus on at least two points: (1) health insurance is a good thing, and (2) our present health insurance system is grossly inadequate and must be improved. Its inadequacy is shown in a single set of statistics. In 1968 personal expenditure for medical care totaled $37.6 billion, of which health insurance covered only $12 billion, 32 percent of the whole. The percentage of medical bills covered represented scant improvement over the 29 percent that had been covered a decade previously and was even *below* the 1967 figure by a percentage point. Clearly, a quantum jump in coverage is required; Walter J. McNerney, president of the Blue Cross Association, believes we must attain 80 to 85 percent of coverage of our medical bills. So do I.

Much coverage makes no sense. For example, some insurers cover minor surgical procedures only when they are performed in the hospital, although they could easily be done in the office. I usually handle this situation by calling the carrier and saying, "If I do this in my office, it will cost you $50. If the patient is admitted to the hospital, your cost will be $250. I'm an easy guy to get along with. Where do you want me to do this operation?"

Insurance coverage is not only inadequate, but it is also hopelessly fragmented. Some 1800 private carriers offer health-care coverage. They vary widely in the benefits they provide; many policies pay scandalously little, a mere spit in the ocean of today's costs. The amount of the premium dollar returned in the form of benefit payments ranges from as low as $.50 with some commercial companies to more than $.90 with Blue Cross plans. The spectrum of exclusions is very wide: a relatively few policies offer really comprehensive coverage at high cost; at the other end you practically have to be bitten by a shark while flying in a commercial airliner to collect anything. Insurers pick and choose among the people they will cover; their inability to insure the low-income, high-risk aged at reasonable cost was directly responsible for Medicare. Part of or all an individual's medical bills may be paid by commercial insurers, nonprofit plans such as Blue Cross, Federal Government plans, the Veterans Administration, local tax money, workman's compensation, a union health center, or a prepaid group practice plan. In addition, there are at least fifteen separate publicly funded programs that provide medical care.

Even the AMA now recognizes that government intervention is necessary. It has proposed a plan that it calls Medicredit, under which individuals would, in effect, receive a public subsidy to enable them to purchase private health insurance. If a family were below a given income level, Government would buy insurance for them. Families above that level would receive full credit against income taxes for health insurance premiums they pay. The tax credit would be reduced as income rises until it disappeared altogether at a certain point of affluence. The plan, to my mind, has three major flaws. It is voluntary. It does not deal with the problem of fragmentation. And it does not touch the present system of delivering medical care except to pump more money into an already heavily overloaded machine, which can only compound a medical inflation now nearing the disaster point.

Nevertheless the AMA stand makes one thing clear: there is no longer any debate over *whether* Government should act; the question now is *what* shall it do?

The answer, I think, has to be some form of compulsory national health insurance. There is much debate about such matters as what part of the cost should be paid out of payroll taxes on employers and employees and what part by Government, whether fiscal intermediaries should be used, and the like. I will leave these matters to others, but one principle I do think vital: the individual's contribution to the cost, whether it be from payroll deductions, like Social Security, through his income tax or in any other way, should be graduated according to his ability to pay.

Comprehensive care will certainly cost several hundred dollars a year per family—a figure that will not hurt the $50,000-a-year man, but that would be an extreme hardship for low-income people.

Further, we should not repeat the mistake that other countries and the Kaiser plan originally made. Experience shows that it is desirable for patients to pay some part of their bills for office visits as a means of cutting down on trivial complaints. Australians pay 10 percent of their medical costs; Frenchmen, 20 percent; Swedes, 25 percent. Kaiser has found it necessary to make a small charge for office visits.

I think the system must be compulsory. I am not willing that a child suffer from lack of medical care because his father either could not buy insurance or was too stupid to do so. Conservatives will label this "Socialistic," just as they did voluntary health insurance years ago. Well, in the depths of the Depression in 1935, the California Medical Association approved, drafted, and had introduced into the State Legislature a bill (S.B. 454) calling for compulsory health insurance to provide comprehensive care. If it was not Socialistic in hard times when doctors' waiting rooms were empty and bills were uncollectible, why is it Socialistic now when those rooms are jammed with waiting patients? If it is not Socialistic to have compulsory insurance for a working man from 9 to 5, why is it Socialistic to cover him for the other hours in the day?

But before health insurance, there must be quality controls on medicine. An unnecessary operation is indefensible no matter how it is paid for. To supply unlimited funds on behalf of the patient with no check on quality is only to encourage the unscrupulous. It would compound chaos.

Medicaid, that well-intentioned mess, is an excellent example of what can happen when a health program is hastily established before we have identified and moved to correct deficiencies in medicine. Improving the quality of care is a first priority.

13

THE TANGLE OF WORMS

The Department of Health, Education and Welfare is hampered by an outdated structure, by facts of size, budget, disparate agencies, bureaus and programs. It has become too unwieldy to carry out its functions with the necessary thrust and responsiveness. HEW needs reorganization, and the sooner the better.

And:

There has never been a formulation of a national health policy as such. In addition, no specific mechanism has been set up to carry out this function. As a consequence, the national health policy is a more or less amorphous set of health goals, which are derived by various means and groups within the Federal structure. Thus the apparent effect of the . . . $20.6 billion budget for fiscal 1971 is to support patterns of health care and service that are outmoded and ineffective, and, in so doing, to compound, rather than help resolve, the current crisis in health care.

The first quotation is from Senator Edward M. Kennedy, the second from the report of a subcommittee headed by Senator Abraham Ribicoff of the Senate Committee on Government Operations. Senator Ribicoff, himself a former secretary of HEW, added, "There are so many programs administered in such bureaucratic confusion that no one—not HEW, not the Bureau of the Budget, not any of the private organizations—was able to tell the subcommittee even how many programs there are."

Thus one sees the tangle of worms in the Federal department that is second only to Defense in size and in the volume of expenditures it controls. The thing is so huge, with so many tentacles crisscrossing and intertwining with one another that few people realize that a genuine and thoroughgoing Federal commitment to the general health is only about three decades old.

As far back as 1778, the Continental Congress established the Marine Hospital Service (which in 1912 became the Public Health Service) to care for the ills of merchant seamen. In 1902 Congress established a Hygienic Laboratory and before World War I mandated it to "study and investigate the diseases of man and conditions influencing the origins and spread thereof." The real birth of most of the modern programs probably began in 1937 with the establishment in Washington of the National Cancer Institute and the authorization for the first time of grants to universities, hospitals, laboratories, or individuals for research. Though it had been envisioned by some planners as early as 1939, a Department of HEW actually came into being only during the Eisenhower Administration.

HEW, of course, became the umbrella for many different health agencies, including the National Institutes of Health. NIH, however, acted rather more like the autonomous relative than the obedient child. Under Dr. James Shannon, an unsurpassed scientist-administrator, NIH had its own pipelines direct to Capitol Hill in the persons of two staunch champions, Senator Lister Hill and Representative John Fogarty; both were chairmen of the respective congressional committees controlling health appropriations. With their enthusiastic encouragement, Federal research funds mounted from $45 million in 1940 to $2.25 billion in 1967—a 5000 percent increase in 27 years. Obviously this kind of exponential growth could not continue indefinitely.

Through its grants-in-aid and work done in its own laboratories, NIH has lifted the United States to world preeminence in biomedical research. Nevertheless there has been some criticism in recent years by medical scientists who deplore an increasing tendency to investigate organ systems rather than diseases, as is the approach of the Institutes of Cancer, Heart and Neurological Diseases. In 1968, under strong pressure from ophthalmologists, Congress carved a new National Eye Institute out of the National Institute of Neurological Diseases and Blindness. The Heart Institute has been expanded to include the lungs; a plan to set up a Kidney Institute is under discussion now.

While there may be some support for such programs among scientists biased toward their special research interests, there is also a great deal of pressure from uninformed laymen. People naturally tend to be much interested in diseases that have seriously affected themselves or their immediate families. A man whose mother has gone blind is far more interested in ocular problems than he is in the liver. It is doubtful that such volunteer agencies as the American Heart Association or the American Cancer Society could survive with anything like their present effectiveness without the ardent support of people whose lives have been touched by those respective diseases.

Congressmen are subject to great pressure from agencies and individuals with such specialized interests (and, indeed, they themselves frequently also have such interests). In addition, almost to a man, they have little scientific background. Obviously no congressman wants to be thought of as so heartless that he will vote against research that might cure or prevent blindness, and most of them are defenseless against exaggerated claims of lives saved and "research already paying for itself." Had Congress turned down the Eye Institute, its members would have been rebuked as "blind to experience"; should they some day balk at an Ear Institute, I suspect they would be assailed as "deaf to hope."

A second sober criticism of NIH rises from the heavy concentration of facilities and talent on its sprawling campus at Bethesda, a suburb of Washington. The scientists who migrate to the lush greenery there further deplete the ranks of medical school faculties. Their brilliance can no longer guide and inspire students. Many of these men tend to become insulated as their memories of teaching and general medical service slip further into the hazy past. There are some men who, for temperamental or other reasons, belong in pure research, but the concentration at Bethesda may be getting out of hand.

Most medical research today is carried out at medical schools, and I think more of it should be. I am not aware that the work is any better done at NIH than it could be done at Johns Hopkins. I know of no discoveries that have been made at NIH that could not also have been made had the same investigators worked on the same problems with the same money at a non-Governmental research center. Do we get any more for our research dollar at Bethesda than we do at Berkeley or Boston? And are we not missing the badly needed abilities of the Bethesda men at our medical schools?

If NIH has its problems, it is at least unlike much of the rest of HEW in being relatively clean of politicking (except when it comes to getting money from Congress), and of the wishful thinking, premature claims, and misleading statistics that too often characterize Federal health pronouncements. Perhaps the prize for pipedreaming ought to go to former President Johnson who, in his 1968 State of the Union message, worried about having to appoint a commission "to study (the) very great problem of an adjustment to a life span and a work span for the average man of 100 years."

The President's worry was premature, to say the least. For all the advances of medical science, we have not appreciably increased the human life span beyond the Biblical three score years and ten. What we have done is to increase our chances of getting to be that old by curing diseases and injuries that formerly would have finished us off at an earlier age. Once we really begin to understand the aging process and to get a real grip on the degenerative diseases, maybe we can find ways of appreciably prolonging life, but I would not count on that happening tomorrow.

One of Washington's worst errors, in my view, is its attempt to decide which diseases are most worthy of the doctor's time and effort. Medical school researchers are perfectly capable of setting up research priorities without the help of Government health officials who are interested in specific diseases or organs. An example of this misguided categorical disease approach was the Heart, Cancer, and Stroke program, midwifed through Congress by

HEW during President Johnson's "honeymoon" period. The bill had its origin in a two-volume report published in December 1964 by a commission headed by Dr. Michael DeBakey, the famous Houston surgeon. An administration bill based on the report was ready for the opening of Congress the following month and was so speedily drafted that it "surprised" HEW Secretary Anthony Celebrezze who conceded that the wording was "vague." Its aim sounded noble enough: to establish at medical schools "centers of excellence" for the treatment of the killer diseases named in its title and through those centers to speed to the practicing physician in the field the very newest discoveries in therapy.

Testimony in support of the bill has been likened to "the manuscript of an off-Broadway play." The only serious opposition came from the AMA, which was still so far in the political doghouse because of its pigheadedness about Medicare that it was not taken seriously. That was ironic; this was one of the few times that the AMA, in an appearance before Congress, was on the side of the angels.

Critics of the categorical approach in the bill were somewhat appeased by the addition of the words "and related diseases" to the title. This added still more vagueness to the already vague language, giving HEW more of what it preferred to call "flexibility." After all, every part of the human body is related to the heart. The footbone is connected to the legbone, the legbone is connected to the thighbone, the thighbone. . . . So after Congress in the fall of 1965 had enacted a watered-down version of the $3 billion program originally requested, less and less was heard about heart, cancer, and stroke, and the title finally gave way altogether in favor of Regional Medical Programs (RMP).

To my mind the entire program was misdirected. Deaths from heart disease, cancer, and stroke predominate among older people. Considering the inevitability of mortality in this age group, it was unrealistic to expect an important extension of life by treating these categories. The DeBakey Commission did not discuss the other causes of death among this group, nor the social costs of merely prolonging the lives—and often prolonging the suffering—of chronically ill old people. If we are really interested in long-term, useful survival, infants and children should be the focal point of our interest, but they have no lobby in Washington.

Senator Warren G. Magnuson has decried recent medical care legislation as "categorical programs, each designated to put one patch on the quilt," and President Johnson himself described the health bills conjured up by HEW as "a programmatic and bureaucratic nightmare." RMP was one more patch on the quilt, one more monster in the nightmare.

The program's aim of educating the practicing physician in the latest developments is hardly likely to accomplish as much as its sponsors hoped. With the proliferation of medical meetings, any doctor who wants to keep up has little difficulty in doing so, while the one who is not interested now very likely will not become much more so. More than mere self-improvement is often offered to lure the doctor to medical meetings. I receive an average of two invitations a day to meetings all over the world and, since the cost of attending one is tax-deductible, many delightful fringe benefits become available. I can attend meetings in Europe or Japan and combine education with low-cost travel. I can attend meetings on a luxury liner to Hawaii and enjoy a sea voyage, courtesy of the Internal Revenue

Service. I can attend meetings and golf at the Homestead, gamble at Las Vegas, sun in Palm Springs, or ski at Aspen. Recently I received the ultimate invitation—a medical meeting combined with an African safari. If I want to be mundane and learn at the least possible cost in money and in time out from practice, there are meetings of my hospital staff with a wide choice of films and TV tapes available and of my county and state professional societies. RMP was hardly needed to give the doctor an opportunity to learn.

My own hospital subscribed to the RMP televised educational programs for a time, but discontinued them. They were good programs, but they were too costly for what they accomplished because they were so ill attended. Some doctors were already familiar with the content; others were just too busy in practice to add yet another meeting to their schedules; some just were not motivated to come. I know of many other hospitals that have also canceled these teaching sessions. This is not necessarily as sad as it seems. As we get more and more specialists who know how to handle difficult cases, there is less need for the general practitioner to know about them. Why, asks the GP, should I attend an educational program about a problem that I would turn over to a specialist anyway while I have an office full of patients clamoring for my time?

Some of the other RMP activities are also duplicative. Such things as televised instruction and consultation, coronary care units, and cooperative arrangements between widely separated institutions all existed long before RMP. Nevertheless, like most government activities, RMP continues to flourish. Conceived in New York by Mary

Lasker, gestated in Houston under the wing of Dr. DeBakey, and prematurely delivered in Washington by the "health establishment," RMP was puny and weak at birth. But the infant has overcome these stigmata and has developed into a lusty, hungry baby. RMP now boasts about 3000 full- and part-time employees, plus 7000 volunteer workers, and has spent $500 million. This is an operation to watch when it attains full growth!

RMP's opportunity to improve the coordination of health services and improve the quality of care was severely compromised when Dr. Dwight L. Wilbur, AMA president, extracted a promise that no "national standards" of medical care were to be imposed. Dr. Robert Q. Marston, then RMP director, specified that the challenge of the program was to "improve the quality of health services without exercising Federal or state governmental control over current patterns of health activities." We have seen what some of the current patterns are.

To confound confusion, Congress in 1966 enacted the "Partnership for Health" law, designed to encourage regional planning for health needs. This program, too, "has no recipe to follow," but invites the "initiative from states and communities." In short order it established itself as a competitor with RMP for scarce planning personnel and funds, further fragmenting authority and adding more overlap. Dr. Philip Lee, then assistant secretary of HEW, admitted that "the present confusion in the planning activities currently under way must be eliminated if we are to benefit from their efforts." As I write, there is a move underway to combine the two bureaucracies, which would be some improvement. Better yet, both programs should have been scrapped. Or would that have been too simplistic a solution? Probably! Federal bureaucracies do not correct poorly designed projects the way the Ford Motor Company handled the Edsel.

Inconsistency abounds in Federal affairs. On the one hand, government goes to great lengths to combat cigarette smoking as the cause of 60,000 deaths a year from lung cancer. On the other, the Department of Agriculture distributes millions of dollars in subsidy to tobacco growers and even spent $210,000 to subsidize a movie, *The World of Pleasure*, which is shown abroad to promote the smoking of cigarettes made with U.S. tobacco.

Important problems are studied to death. As a form of procrastination there is nothing to equal a study by a task force. As soon as that august body turns in its report, a new blue-ribbon commission is formed to do the same job all over again. The same stilted recommendations are made repeatedly by the same people. As Dr. Irvine Page has put it, "The recurrence of these names becomes monotonous." He marvels at how "they seem to move with even grace from Committee A to Committee Z, regardless of the task at hand." Senator John J. Williams once suggested sarcastically to the then HEW secretary, John Gardner, that he name a "task force on task forces."

The Government often refuses to lead. The Planned Parenthood organization fought for years on behalf of family planning, while Government sat on its hands because politicians feared reprisals from Catholic voters. As late as 1966, long after most people had recognized the need for family planning, HEW was still telling a congressional committee that it did not favor a positive Federal position on the subject. Only when the pressure became overwhelming was HEW at last prodded into a more enlightened attitude. This is not leadership.

Finally, there is the constant intrusion of ward-heeling politics into many matters where it does not belong. Aside from the family planning example I have just given, there is the even more notorious instance of the refusal of President Nixon to permit HEW Secretary Robert Finch to appoint Dr. John H. Knowles assistant secretary because the AMA opposed him. There was no question about Dr. Knowles's superlative abilities or even his political credentials. (He had actively worked for Nixon in the preceding campaign.) He was simply too outspoken about our health problems to suit the right wing of organized medicine.

The same sort of politicking with health goes on at the state level. One of Ronald Reagan's first acts as governor of California was to fire highly capable and widely respected Dr. Lester Breslow as director of Public Health. Dr. Breslow's offense? "He does not fit in with my philosophy."

And what was the governor's "philosophy?" Reagan's election swept into office with him all but one of the Republican statewide candidates. The defeated one was Spencer Williams. Reagan had announced that he would name only men of the highest caliber to appointive office, and he actually appointed a special committee to find a new Health and Welfare administrator. One day the committee was deliberating over a list of five names when one of the governor's lieutenants walked in and said, "Spencer Williams (a lawyer with no real background or training in either health or welfare) has a great interest in health and welfare." The committee got the message. Forthwith, Williams' name was added to the list, the other five were eliminated, and Williams got the job. I have a "great interest" in football. I wonder if I should apply for the job of head coach of the Los Angeles Rams. Four years later, health and welfare in California is a disgraceful "mess." Perhaps on-the-job training is not appropriate for the head man of a department with a budget of $1.5 billion per year.

I have had my own experiences with politics in health matters. In March 1966 I was in Washington as a special consultant to Dr. Ellen Winston, then commissioner of welfare, when I was invited to an "important meeting" in her office attended by half a dozen Presidential appointees. The topic turned out to be the "pacification" of the South Vietnamese countryside. The purpose, I soon found, was to devise programs of high visibility that could be put into effect by June—three months away.

Even assuming the plans could be perfected and the vast, creaking Federal machine moved in that time—an obvious impossibility—there was another barrier: the Viet Cong controlled most of the countryside, especially at night. I listened in utter amazement as the most fantastic, utterly unrealistic notions were bandied about. There was a real Alice-in-Wonderland air to some of the suggestions that everyone else seemed to be taking with deadly seriousness.

Finally, Dr. Winston, noting that I had some experience in Southeast Asia, called on me. I pointed out that the proposals were unrealistic and asked whether the decisions being made were scientific or political. There was a long silence; finally, the surgeon general, sitting on my right, said, "This meeting is politically inspired." I promptly replied that, not being a politician, I feared I had nothing to contribute, and I withdrew from further discussion. Come June, right on schedule, President Johnson announced to the world that in the case of pacification, "We are beginning to hang some coon skins on the wall." Where he got the coon skins I still do not know.

At about that time, I was asked by Douglass Cater, a Presidential assistant, to prepare a position paper on family planning. (On my trips to Washington, I usually conferred at the White House with Mr. Cater who was the President's chief liaison with HEW.) I wrote it out in a frank and realistic manner, and one of Dr. Winston's secretaries typed it for me. Unknown to me, she showed my report to the commissioner, though it was not meant for her. Dr. Winston called me in. "You have a personal relationship with Doug Cater, so I suppose you can send something like this in," she said. "But I want to point out that it's on HEW stationery and Federal bureaucrats don't write as bluntly as this. I'll send it through only on the basis of your personal relationship with Cater." She did so, but it was clear that this was the second time within a week that I had caused her some embarrassment.

At this time I was being considered for the position of the full-time director of the Medicaid program within HEW. My introduction to Dr. Winston had been arranged by both Secretary Gardner and Assistant Secretary Lee, and I knew the FBI was working on my clearance. Dr. Winston called me into her office to say, "Dr. Gerber, I'm sure you would be unhappy and we would be unhappy if you became a Washington bureaucrat. For the good of both of us, I would rather that you just serve as my personal consultant." That is what happened, and a little while later Dr. Francis L. Land was appointed to the Medicaid post. It was the best thing that could have happened to me. In retrospect, if I had been in Frank Land's position, I would have gone stark, staring bonkers.

I have few answers to Washington's problems. Perhaps the sheer size and nature of the Federal bureaucracy make some of them insoluble. But I firmly believe that at the very least we could work out a national health policy, with a coherent listing of our priorities and some reasonably coordinated strategy for fulfilling them.

14

A DIFFERENT DRUMMER. . . .

In recent years—the medical profession has been freely criticized for self-interest and neglect of public duty. Without doubt, in my opinion, there has been some substance in these criticisms, but the main factor working against the effectiveness of them has been the hollow note in the voices of those who make them. When we hear the wharves humming with happy shouts of the Sunday workers proudly turning the ships around to get the butter more quickly to the Old Country—when the coal-getters ask leave to work on a holiday rather than let the national bunkers get low—when the politician resigns rather than be party to a political bribe or favor contrary to the public welfare—then these criticisms of the doctors will make more impression. In fact, as rackets go, the medical one has never been a particularly harmful one.

Winston Churchill

I dare say Churchill would have responded in similar vein to accusations that our health service is a nonsystem. How many of our institutions are more efficient? The Federal Government? The army? We know how Ralph Nader rates General Motors and how our rioting students rate the universities from which much of the criticism of our health service comes. When others improve their own systems, the "criticisms of the doctors will make more impression."

Medicine is being told that we are not enough concerned with the community and must enter "a new era— the community era." Some planners see the prototype of the future in the neighborhood health centers that are operated through the Office of Economic Opportunity. The centers were opened in rosy clouds of glowing promise. The *Los Angeles Times* hoped for great things from the Watts center:

> Everybody is to have a family physician who is backed up by surgeons, dentists, social workers, psychiatrists, laboratories and everything else needed to give comprehensive outpatient care. Instead of patients traveling from one office to another in various parts of the city, the specialists come to the neighborhood center where the patient lives. Furthermore, they do it at times of the day or night that are convenient to the needs of the patient.

The article went on to quote the OEO's Dr. Gary London: "The new system allows people to have a major say in deciding what kind of services they get and when and where they get them. We're not claiming yet that we've found the ideal system. We're still searching for it. But when we find it for one group—the poor—might it not be effective for all?" Others have also asked that question. Even the AMA's Council on Medical Service concluded, although with several "ifs," that the OEO centers might have an application "to the problems of medical care economics for the middle-income group as well."

Heaven forbid! Two months after the *Los Angeles Times* piece just quoted, the paper ran another article by its medical editor, Harry Nelson, headed: "Watts Health

Clinic Beset by Multitude of Problems." The second article cited financial troubles, shortages of professional personnel, and "vicious infighting" for power among the nonprofessionals. In a separate context, Drs. Milton Davis and Robert Tranquada, of the University of Southern California School of Medicine, with which the Watts center is affiliated, noted that "while the OEO, the university and the people of the community may want health services, they have different experiences and different priorities." It is these differences and struggles for power that have resulted in serious conflicts between the centers and local community boards, between community boards and sponsoring organizations (e.g., medical schools), between members of community boards, between professionals and lay workers, and between ethnic groups—blacks and Spanish-Americans.

The fetish for community control—"maximum feasible participation by the unknowledgeable"—has led to many a problem. The Lincoln Hospital Mental Health Service in the Bronx, New York, began with starry eyed dreams. The state of euphoria persisted for several years, and outside investigators were so ridiculously unaware of the inner turmoil at Lincoln Center that it was honored with the American Psychiatric Association's "Silver Achievement Award." Its director, Dr. Harris B. Peck, philosophized: "When there is a foot planted in the seat of my trousers to kick me out of here, I'll know we have succeeded. It will mean that the people want to take over the running of their own community, and that's the way it should be." The foot was planted soon enough. A later article on the center in *Medical Tribune* began: "A community-based health institution, perhaps the most widely known of its kind in the nation, recently exploded in bitter recrimination, wildcat work stoppages, the temporary ouster from his office of the physician who directs the project and demands that he and his two chief assistants resign." "The program," the article continued, "is in a state of chaos." And at the Gouverneur Center in New York, the conflict between the community and the administration generated such a white heat that, for a time, the center required 24-hour police protection.

Surely middle-income people may be forgiven for not wanting to dive into this particular mainstream of health service! Fortunately for the public, surgical residents, unlike the "community," do not take over operations when they think they are ready, but only when their chiefs think they are. Even then the seniors are not booted out of the operating room; they stay until they are certain nothing has gone awry.

I myself work in a neighborhood health center that serves people of all kinds, except that we call our center a group practice clinic. Neither patients nor representatives of the community tell us what to do. They have no voice in the way we practice medicine, the days we open, the hours we work, the design of our building, the furniture we buy, or the personnel we hire (all of whom, naturally, are from the community). Yet we are swamped with patients who must be satisfied; 90 percent of them are referred by other patients. Why should a center be different because all the people of the neighborhood are poor and uneducated? The public makes no unreasonable demands upon plumbers; I do not see that any community, rich or poor, has the right to kick the doctors around. The ghetto poor have problems of employment and racial discrimination, but wrecking medical institutions will not solve them.

The neighborhood health centers have plenty of other troubles. Though the physical surroundings are usually far more attractive and comfortable than they are in old-fashioned clinics, many basic problems remain, and new ones have been added. Medical personnel are in as short supply at the centers as elsewhere, and in some places important specialties are not represented at all. Patients are given appointments, instead of just being told to come in and wait, but it often happens that part-time doctors, busy in their private offices elsewhere, keep them waiting anyway. On the other hand, fully 30 percent of the patients do not show up for their appointments, thus leaving the doctor waiting. Physicians are often forced to spend endless weary hours in conferences with social workers, nurse practitioners, urban anthropologists, and community representatives, wasting much precious professional time. Not all centers are winning spectacular local acceptance; some are used by fewer than 50 percent of the eligible population. As Dr. Arthur Coleman, medical director of San Francisco's Hunters Point-Bayview center, explained, "The mere establishment of a physical plant will not greatly alter the behavior of large masses of poor people. A shining example of this is public housing." Nor are the centers necessarily economical. Governor Russell Peterson of Delaware asserted that neighborhood center care costs more than twice as much as the same services provided at a physician's office.

Here is what a "compassionate, concerned pediatrician" had to say about his 15-month experiences at an OEO center in a letter to the editor of the *New England Journal of Medicine*:

> Although the aims and goals of the OEO health center were admirable, things just didn't work. I had file clerks who couldn't file, telephone operators who couldn't properly answer the telephone, and so forth. The morale of our entire staff was deplorable. Although the plans for the center called for eight full-time pediatricians, after I left there was only one full-time pediatrician and a half-time foreign doctor with questionable training. There were a few other doctors who came in and took a clinic part-time. But the care the people received tended to be somewhat depersonalized and fragmented. They didn't seem to appreciate the care nor to enjoy it; neither did we. Evidence of their dissatisfaction can be seen from the clinic attendance figures—only about 30 percent kept their appointments. Yet the cost to the government for each patient visit probably was far in excess of $50, because I know the pro-rata of my salary for each patient visit was over $20.

Early enthusiasts hoped to blanket the country with as many as 1000 OEO centers, each serving about 20,000 people. That would require 20,000 physicians and at least double that number of other health workers. Where would these people come from? What is there in our past experience to encourage the quixotic idea that 20,000 doctors, whose economic health has never been better, will give up lucrative practices to take comparatively low-salaried positions among the poor? There will always be some selfless and saintly doctors ready to yield the pleasures of affluence and accept the frustrations of working in urban and rural slums, but their number is relatively small. With a shortage of 350,000 paramedical personnel, how will these centers compete for the nonexistent health worker? Dr. Herbert Adams, director of Boston's Lahey Clinic, has noted this "glaring defect of government medicine. The tendency is always to legislate a good program, but to give insufficient thought to providing the facilities and manpower to implement it."

It may be that I have overemphasized the dark side of the picture of OEO medicine. Without doubt there are many capable and dedicated people working in the centers and giving good quality care to people who badly need it. Indeed, the Watts Center in Los Angeles has shown a remarkable improvement in patient acceptance and quality of medical care (while the situation in Lincoln Hospital in New York has gone from bad to worse). If my remarks have been one-sided, however, it is for the purpose of calling attention to the fact that neighborhood health centers are not the answer to everyone's health problems as some naive health officials at HEW would have us believe. Objective, outside evaluations of neighborhood health centers are infrequent. Occasionally one appears. Dr. Samuel Standard, clinical professor of Surgery at NYU Medical School, surveyed the surgical service at the Gouverneur neighborhood center in lower Manhattan. After looking at the report by the doctors connected with the center, Dr. Standard flatly stated, "The hiatus between these statements and my findings is so large I wonder if we are occupying the same planet." Dr. Standard's analysis may not have been completely objective, but at least his views did not have the usual heavy sugar coating of Government reports.

Those who would make deep-seated changes in our health-care system are not concerned solely with the poor.

For example, Dr. Martin Cherkasky, director of New York's Montefiore Hospital and Medical Center, vigorously advocates phasing out private practice, with its "piece-work" fee-for-service reimbursement of physicians. He would replace the system with a system of hospital-based group practices and would put the doctors on "handsome" salaries.

Dr. Cherkasky's suggested solution suffers from inflexi-bility. When quality standards are kept high, hospital-based group practice is an excellent method of providing services, but it does not fit the needs of *all* patients and *all* doctors. A monolithic system would not even neces-sarily improve the care received by the poor. We have supposedly uniform systems of public education, but will anyone seriously contend that the children of Watts attend schools as good as those of Beverly Hills?

Further, with the present physician shortage, the need to retain the fee-for-service incentive is important. In gen-eral, salaried physicians do not work as long hours nor see as many patients as do the nonsalaried practitioners. The former have little incentive to work more than a 40-hour week; the latter often work 60 or 70 hours. A switch to a system of all salaried physicians would only compound the problem of too heavy a demand for insufficient existing manpower.

There is yet another problem. Not all doctors march to the same drummer. Doctors differ in their abilities, experi-ence, and temperament. I have been in group practice too long not to know that there are many physicians who can-not practice at their best—and some who cannot practice at all—in such an arrangement. Group members must work as a team, but some men are just constitutionally unable to do that. Such a man has to be the quarterback, calling every play. He may be a fine doctor, however; I, and members of my family, receive part of our medical attention from men who do not feel that they could function well in group practice.

I hold out for a pluralistic approach to health care; there is more than one route to the goal. There is room under our system for solo practitioners, medical partnerships, and multispecialty group practices, both fee-for-service and prepaid. It would be unwise to force a single system of medical care on the heterogenous American public and the fiercely independent American physician. Both patient and doctor should have a free choice, always remembering that that choice should be as informed as possible and that quality controls must restrict medical entrepreneurs who would use the free economy to victimize the uninformed. It is true that many people now get high quality care without having free choice. Members of the armed forces and patients at VA hospitals have little, if any, opportunity to choose among physicians. The person who goes to the Mayo Clinic has little choice; he is usually assigned by the clinic to the doctor or team of doctors judged most qualified to handle his case. But if Mayo Clinic standards were the rule in this country, and if the Mayo patient were the paradigm of the whole population, this book would not have been necessary. Until the day comes when that is true, I shall continue to agree with the statement of Isidor Falk, the "father of Social Security": "Instead of being derisive and critical of those who have been prominently identified with advocating the principle of 'free choice of doctor,' I suggest that we should increasingly encourage the development of parallel patterns of service systems, and we should advocate that people have a free choice."

No one system can possibly please everybody. In both England and Sweden, despite the excellent national systems of health care, there are many patients who prefer to go to private doctors and pay the extra cost out of pocket. In England there are so many such patients that private health insurance systems, comparable to our Blue Cross-Blue Shield, are flourishing. At the same time, many doctors have become disenchanted with the health service, and it is not unusual to read in the British Medical press such comments as, "There has been no more sophisticated ideal and undertaking than the Health Service, but no social asset so undermined by its intrinsic liabilities." Small wonder, then, that an appreciable number of British doctors are emigrating so that the government has serious worries about its "brain drain" and has even conducted advertising campaigns in the United States and in Commonwealth countries trying to lure British physicians home again. We have much to learn from the British about medical care quality, but little about health-care organization.

Here at home the group practice arrangement that I prefer has not worked for everybody, either. The Rip Van Winkle Clinic, an excellent group in Hudson, New York, folded in 1964 after eighteen years and despite subsidies of more than $1 million from philanthropists who were anxious to demonstrate the value of comprehensive group practice in a rural setting. It failed for two principal reasons: not enough patients accepted it, and there was dissension among the doctors. There are other such examples.

I take a jaundiced view of Washington's thrust to "reshape" medical organization and improve doctors' "efficiency" by pushing them all into prepaid group practice. Even the founder of the Kaiser Health Plan, Dr. Sidney Garfield, freely admits that prepaid group practice "is far from being the entire answer." It may also come as a surprise to some in Washington that most solo men no longer work in antiquated, dusty offices above the corner drugstore. More and more they are improving their efficiency by moving into medical arts centers with modern facilities, often conveniently near hospitals. They are joining other physicians in a like specialty to form two-, three-, or four-men partnerships that provide very adequate service 24 hours a day.

In Washington itself, not very far from HEW headquarters, internist Dr. Michael Halberstam seems content to practice in a one-man office:

> Meantime, I continue to practice by myself, tucked away in a cozy office, and turning out patients the way Aran Islanders turn out sweaters—one by one. Since I am neither more callous nor more stupid than most, why do I persist in such an archaic method? The reason is that medicine still often amounts to one man asking another for help. In many (but not all) fields of medicine, effectiveness depends on a deep and continuing personal relationship between healer and patient.

It must be comforting for a patient to meet a man who speaks like that. Surely he does not think of himself as part of the health-service *industry*, of his patients as *consumers of care*, nor of their families as *social units*, and I find it impossible to believe that his patients think of him as a *vendor* of service. The practice arrangement that Dr. Halberstam chooses is to me less important than his philosophy. I know that whenever I am sick, I want a man like him to take care of me.

Neither group nor solo practice has much new to offer people in really rural communities. Our superb highway system does help to mitigate their problem; a farmer may drive a much greater distance to see his doctor and still get there quicker than does his city cousin fighting traffic congestion in the polluted air. Those who live in very remote areas will always have a medical care problem, no matter what the system. Perhaps public health nurses, when we can get enough of them, can man health stations in some isolated communities, but there will always be a few people so far out that they had better stay healthy, depend upon helicopters, or move closer to civilization.

15

OUR WORST DISEASE—POVERTY

LIKE any scarce commodity in a free market, medical care is rationed according to ability to pay. Thus the poor, who need it most, get the least of it. It does not matter who they are—Mexican-Americans in a California migrant labor camp, blacks in the Chicago ghetto, whites in the back woods of Appalachia, or Indians in a remote corner of Arizona—the poor are sick; they are not in a state of "social well-being."

By the niggardly definitions of the Federal Government —a family of four living on an annual income of $4,345 —there are 45 million Americans classed as poor or near-poor, and the figure does not include 2 million economically deprived people who live in institutions nor yet another 3 million whose own incomes are below the poverty line but who live with more fortunate relatives. Most members of racial minorities are poor or near poor, but most of the poor are not members of racial minorities; two out of three poor individuals are white; so are four out of five of the near poor. About 40 percent of the poor are children under sixteen.

The physical problems of the poor are appalling. In the

black ghetto of Detroit's Near East Side the infant mortality rate of 69 per 1000—United States average: 22.1 per 1000—is on a par with that of Costa Rica. In Bolivar County, Mississippi, the maternal death rate among poor Negroes is 15.3 per 1000, compared to 2.1 among white women. In some areas of the Navajo reservation, both infant mortality and the incidence of tuberculosis are seven times the national rate. For some common infectious diseases, the incidence is up to ten times the national rate.

"More than fourteen million Americans have total incomes, including welfare, which virtually guarantee that they will be malnourished; 23.6 million more have incomes that put them in serious danger of being malnourished," according to Senator George McGovern. Among the proven medical effects of malnutrition are premature birth, increased infant mortality, stunted physical growth, anemia, and permanent brain damage. The Bureau of the Budget has estimated what it costs this country to care for just those ills that are caused by malnutrition; it amounts to $3.30 for every dollar that it would take to feed all these people. "It costs three times as much to maintain malnutrition as it would to end it," Senator McGovern said.

According to the National Center for Health Statistics, in families earning more than $7000 a year, 11.9 persons per 1000 have heart conditions severe enough to restrict daily activity; in families with incomes of less than $2000, the figure is 53.8 persons per 1000. Comparable figures for other ailments: mental and nervous conditions, 4.2 versus 26.4; arthritis and rheumatism, 8.7 versus 59.3; high blood pressure, 3.9 versus 23.8; orthopedic impairments, 14.9 versus 54.4; and visual impairments, 2.7 versus 23.4. These horrifying figures should make clear why I regard *poverty itself as our worst disease.*

Those are some of the medical aspects of poverty. I need not detail the familiar social aspects: the breakup of families (a quarter of all poor families are headed by women), illegitimacy rates that approach 50 percent in some areas, rampant juvenile delinquency, and rising crime rates. The dollar costs of welfare—Federal, state, and local—are currently increasing at the rate of $3 billion per year. In the city of New York alone, more than one person out of every eight is on welfare, some of them third-generation descendants of people who went on relief during the Depression. The city had 1,077,989 persons receiving some form of welfare aid as of June 1970, 10 percent of the national total. Boston and Baltimore are not far behind with 11.5 percent and 10.8 percent of their respective populations receiving welfare. In Los Angeles the number of aid to dependent children cases rose 293 percent between 1960 and 1969, and the number of welfare cases is currently increasing by 20,000 each month. Most tragically, the welfare check has replaced the job-holding father for more than 6 million children in this country.

Poverty feeds upon itself. The poor marry earlier, have babies sooner, and have more of them. Minuscule incomes can afford neither the living space nor the food that large families require. The children receive an inferior education, and they grow up mentally, physically, and emotionally stunted, unable to improve their lot. This is the vicious cycle that perpetuates poverty from generation to generation.

Like others, we doctors want to cure the disease of poverty, if we only knew how. No medical school could possibly make us both competent in our own profession and expert in all the complexities of education, slum housing, unemployment, and racial discrimination. It will take a lot of people to cure this disease. Exterminators can do more about rat bites than doctors can. Legislators appropriating money can do more about malnutrition. Physicians can only treat a slum child who has been poisoned by the lead paint in his slum apartment; society must eliminate the hazard. Unable to cure the fundamental disease, the doctor must content himself with the less satisfactory task of treating the symptoms, the ailments of the poor.

The Tachi Indians live on a California reservation of 180 acres. All are on welfare—miserable families who live in cardboard shacks without electricity, running water, or indoor toilets. The place stinks of garbage and excrement. A Quaker group gave the Tachis a three-room schoolhouse, including a fully equipped kitchen. The Tachis promptly stripped the building and burned it for firewood. The Tachi children are indescribably dirty, infested with lice and continually ill with dysentery, colds, and pneumonia. Tuberculosis is rampant. The Tachis are very sick people. What do they need? Doctors?

It is not easy for the poor to find high quality care. We have previously looked at the maldistribution of physicians; one result is that the physicians who have remained to practice among the poor are so much in demand and so overworked that they are seldom able to give a patient the time and thoughtful attention he deserves. The poor frequently receive "mass production" care from "production line" doctors, many of whom are foreign trained. Dr. Roger Egeberg met a physician who sees 80 patients a

day and inquired, "Tell me, do you give 'em time to drop
their pants before you give 'em the penicillin shot?" In the
hands of the less conscientious doctors, such assembly line
medicine can be very profitable. *Medical Economics* told
of a Chicago slum practitioner who allows each patient
exactly three minutes for a charge of $10, thus averaging
$200 an hour. Asked how he can even make a diagnosis in
that time, the magazine said he shrugged and replied, "If
I miss them the first time, I get them the second time, or
the third." All of which may help to explain why, when a
poor person says he is sick, someone in his family is likely
to ask anxiously, "Yes, but are you sick $10 worth?"

The attitudes and ignorance of the poor constitute a
formidable barrier to improving their health care. Drs.
Lawrence Bergner and Alonza Yerby summarize their
findings in New York:

> The poor behave differently from the middle class and
> the affluent across a wide spectrum related to health
> care. Illness is defined differently. There is less accurate
> health information. The poor are less inclined to take pre-
> ventive measures and delay longer in seeking medical
> care. When they do approach health practitioners, they
> are more likely to seek subprofessionals or the marginal
> practitioners often found in their neighborhoods. It ap-
> pears that the people most in need of medical services are
> the ones who least often obtain them.

The ignorance of the poor often militates against the
health of others besides themselves. Fluoridation of public water supplies benefits the poor more than the affluent,
because they have less access to dental care, but it helps
the children of all classes. Yet in one public opinion sampling, fluoridation was favored by only 13 percent of those

with less than six years of education, but by 68 percent of those who had at least entered college. According to another survey, only 28 percent of those who had not graduated from high school even knew what the purpose of fluoridation was, though 81 percent of college graduates did. Small wonder then that when referenda are held on fluoridating water supplies, all too often the ignorance of the poor, allied with the bigotry of some, emerge victorious over the health of all the town's children.

Medicaid, which Dr. John H. Knowles has accurately called "an abortion," has fairly well destroyed the myth that the only thing standing between the poor and good quality care is the ability to pay. Passing a law does not change "the culture of poverty," and in most states Medicaid has done little to improve the care received by the poor. For the medically unsophisticated, a system that offers no protection against quacks and guarantees no standard of service makes a sour joke of the words "free choice." The truth is that the free choice exists, not for the patient, but only for the doctor, who exercises it by choosing not to practice in urban or rural slums.

This being the hard fact, we had better recognize its inevitable corollary, that we cannot in the immediate future realistically offer the poor all the amenities now enjoyed by the affluent. The resources to provide them do not exist. To promise the poor pie in the sky is only to encourage rising expectations and thus to fertilize even greater frustration when those hopes are dashed, as they surely must be.

We tend to lose sight of the fact that the culture of poverty may determine the quality of care the poor receive as much as does the particular system under which it is

rendered. British authorities, as recently as 1970, acknowledged that their poor do not fare as well under socialized
medicine as the more affluent: "We have learned from 15
years experience of the Health Service that the higher income groups know how to make better use of the service;
they tend to receive more specialized attention; occupy
more of the beds in better equipped and staffed hospitals;
receive more elective surgery; have better maternal care
and are more likely to get psychiatric help and psycho-
therapy than low income groups." It is crystal clear and I
cannot stress too strongly that equality of medical care will
not be possible under any health system—whether in
Communist Russia, Socialist England, or capitalistic America until there is equality of income, education, and
sophistication.

How, then, can we best provide medical care for the
poor? In the same way as in every other country! When
their economic level is raised, lower-income groups automatically seek and obtain a higher level of medical care.
The surest answer to the problem of substandard care is a
vigorous campaign to eliminate poverty. Simply put, a
steady, well-paying job will do far more to improve a
poor man's health than a neighborhood health center with
its doctors and drugs.

But what should we be doing in the meanwhile? Realistically speaking, poverty will not be abolished for a long
time in a country that sets higher priorities on wars and
moonshots than on grappling with poverty here at home.
And as long as we are being realistic, let's not be pipe-
dreamers about "mainstream" care for the poor. They
obviously will require their own health service system.

In one sense, they have long had such a system. Tradi-

tionally, when they have been served at all, the poor have
been served either as charity patients of an individual physician or in the wards and clinics of public hospitals. Many
voluntary hospitals, too, serve the poor to the limit that it
is financially and physically possible for them. The country
is laced with a network of county and municipal hospitals
(in the case of Louisiana, state hospitals) that have in the
past delivered fairly satisfactory, good quality service to
those who could not afford private care. A generation ago
it was commonplace to hear, "The rich and the poor get
the best medical care." It was the man in the middle, then
without health insurance, who could not pay for costly
care and was ashamed or ineligible to take public care.
The poor in the big cities were fortunate in being able to
turn to world-famous hospitals, like Bellevue, Boston City,
or Cook County. The rural poor were out of sight. Indeed,
it is highly questionable if accurate data were kept of the
incidence of diesase and the causes of death in the hollows
of Appalachia or the back roads of the deep South.

For years now, the city center and the public hospital
that serves it have been rotting. As the neighborhood
turned into a slum, the paint at the hospital began to peel,
the plaster to fall. As the upper- and middle-income people moved out into the suburbs and were replaced by the
poor, so the burden thrown onto the public hospital grew.
The health gap between the affluent and the poor gradually widened. The newborn mortality rate was only 9 percent higher for nonwhites than for whites in 1935; 30 years
later, the figure was 60 percent. There has been no help
from the private sector: not a single new voluntary hospital has been built in a city center for more than twenty
years.

Nor did public support grow in proportion to the burden. There were other and squeakier wheels clamoring for the municipal grease. Overflowing schools, mushrooming welfare rolls, improved police and fire protection, and better sanitation all had their advocates down at City Hall demanding and getting more money. Public employees, long underpaid, wanted and got better salaries. (Some years ago public employees in Chicago won a 10 percent raise. Deadpan, the administration increased the salaries of interns at Cook County Hospital from $12 to $13.20 a month.) There was no effective counterbalancing pressure on behalf of the public hospitals. For the poor, health ranks in priority behind such more immediately pressing matters as jobs, housing, and schools; doctors and administrators who spoke up for the public hospitals had little political clout. Politicians lost interest in public hospitals for two more reasons: in times of prosperity, full employment, and much higher wages elsewhere, there were no longer as many Brownie points to be won by getting jobs in public hospitals for constituents; with health care increasingly being regarded as the right of everyone, the politician was no longer doing a voter any big favor by getting him into the hospital. If there is no political profit in it, why bother?

Population shifts also created other problems. New slums opened up far from the public hospitals. Los Angeles County Hospital was built in East Los Angeles to serve the low-income Mexican-Americans living there, which was right for the time. Then Watts sprang up—ten miles and three bus rides away. (The same factors have also created severe problems for many of our prestigious voluntary and university hospitals. I have already mentioned how Temple University lost $800,000 in 1969 on the services its hospital supplied to the poor blacks who have become its neighbors.)

So our public hospitals have fallen into a state of disgraceful decay. Many people are aware of the problems of the hospital in their own community and think that perhaps they are unique because they do not know that the same thing is happening elsewhere. Far from being unique or even unusual to any one place, the plight of our public hospitals is a severe national problem. In recent years there have been frightful convulsions over the public hospitals in New York, Boston, Chicago, Los Angeles, New Orleans, Houston, Washington, and Kansas City, to name a few examples. There have been bitter battles between doctors seeking support for the hospitals and tightfisted politicians, "exposés" of patronage and "snakepit" conditions, threats of medical staff strikes, and closure of badly needed wards because there was not money enough to operate them. In Los Angeles, interns and residents actually sued the county and hospital administration in an attempt to alleviate overcrowding. Boston City Hospital and Kansas City General lost their accreditations; a hassle between the Chicago politicians and the house staff at Cook County almost emptied the hospital and shook it to its foundations.

In view of the vast manpower shortage, the best thing we can do for the poor right now is to improve our public hospitals and make maximum use of them. Assembly line methods are inescapable, no matter what we do. Using the public hospitals at least assures that the poor enter facilities that turn out a superior health-care product. If it requires an outpouring of Federal money to beef up and improve the public hospitals, and I think it decidedly does, there is at least no other place where we can get better value for the health-care dollar.

It is not only the inpatient services that are important; we need also to strengthen both outpatient clinics and emergency services. Many of the objectionable features of the old clinics can be easily eliminated with a little money and effort. It is no great trick to make forbidding waiting rooms with their wooden benches into comfortable, attractive places. Clinic floors do not have to be covered with dirt and vermin. Branch clinics can be built out in the slum areas and, if closely coordinated with the main hospital, would certainly be an improvement over a freestanding neighborhood health center.

Garages can be established in slum areas where ambulances can be stationed to assure a quick trip to the hospital in emergencies. A few cities here have such a system; so does Moscow. Emergency rooms should be beefed up to the maximum possible. The ER is by far the fastest growing hospital service today. The numbers of the poor who use it as a family doctor is increasing steadily, but so is its use by the more affluent. As more sympathetic people are beginning to recognize that the doctor is really entitled to an unbroken night's sleep now and then and to a little relaxation with his family, they are turning to the emergency room at off-times with problems that are not major, but that do require prompt medical attention.

Those well-regulated voluntary and university hospitals that are willing to give community service to the poor should be encouraged in every way to do so. Certainly, at a bare minimum, the full cost of such service should be borne by government. There is no reason why the bills of the poor should be paid by overcharging other patients.

The ills of the poor concern us all: we all should pay the
bill through taxes.

The urban poor are accustomed to their public hospitals.
Black southern migrants in the Chicago slums have an infant mortality rate 50 percent higher than long-time residents of the same slums; apparently they have brought
Mississippi ways with them, while the oldtimers have
learned the health-care ropes. In Los Angeles, many poor
residents continue to travel the long way to the county
hospital clinics. The hospital recently opened a new outpatient building which the county thought would satisfy
its needs for years to come; instead the clinics are already
so overcrowded that patients are waiting two to four
weeks for appointments or routine x-ray examinations.
Medicaid was supposed to empty the public hospitals by
diverting patients to mainstream care, but most are as
crowded as ever, and in many, patients are spilling out
into the halls.

Public hospitals *can* be improved. In Minneapolis, authorities were thinking of shutting down the ancient and
ramshackle Hennepin County General Hospital, but they
found that despite their long-standing tradition of offering
welfare recipients free choice of hospitals, more of them
were coming to Hennepin County than ever before. The
hospital was also still badly needed for the two traditional
raisons d'être of such places: as the "hospital of last resort,"
the place where anyone could come any time and be sure
of treatment, and as a medical training center (10 percent
of all Minnesota doctors have been trained there). Fortunately, as the hospital's administrator, Paul J. Vogt, put it,
"We've got a bright young county board here, not the
bunch of old fossils you find in some places. They've dis-

covered that health can be a good thing." They let the community in on the discovery, too, and a citizens committee was organized. It pushed for a $25 million bond issue to build the hospital a complete new plant and won the referendum by a 10–1 margin. The hospital is also reorganizing itself internally, and is well along the road toward becoming a full-fledged medical center which will offer the whole range of comprehensive services. Is Hennepin County alone? Public hospitals in Seattle and San Diego have been reorganized, affiliated with medical schools, and are taking new leases on life, as well as changing the old image of county hospital to the new one of university hospital.

Some people see an emerging pattern for rural care in the Tufts-Delta Health Center at Mound Bayou, Mississippi. There, under the energetic direction of Dr. H. Jack Geiger of Tufts Medical School, a group of professionals is working to improve the health of 14,000 abjectly poor blacks. Their work is as much socioeconomic as it is medical; for example, to fight malnutrition they started a cooperative farm and a cannery. ("We're the only health center in the country that's got tractors in the budget," Dr. Geiger likes to say.) While I look with honest admiration at the dedication and selflessness of the staff, I simply cannot believe that this pattern will be widely copied. That degree of dedication is too rare; unhappily, there just are not enough men like Jack Geiger.

Staffing will be a continuing problem at both urban hospitals and in rural areas. As Elkham Lahav of the University of Connecticut School of Medicine aptly put it, "In a free society, distribution of professional manpower is predominantly a function of personal decisions made by individual practitioners, and choices of practice locations result from the personal benefits they—rather than their potential clientele—expect to derive." Improved public hospitals will provide more attractive working and training conditions for doctors, and I would expect that most of the work in them will be done by interns and residents, supervised by a core of extremely well-paid attending physicians. The more undesirable the location and conditions, the higher salaries must be: in the Navy, submarine duty pays extra.

To get doctors out into even less desirable rural areas may require even more drastic action. Mexico and other Latin American countries now require that every young physician serve a tour of duty among the rural disadvantaged before moving on to the practice location of his choice. Since the Federal and state governments are now paying by far the largest part of the cost of the doctor's education, I do not feel it unreasonable to ask the doctor to pay his debt by serving the unfortunate for a time. The AMA and the Association of American Medical Colleges moved in this direction when they suggested that such service might be recognized as an acceptable substitute for military service under the draft. Late in 1970, President Nixon signed into law a measure establishing a National Health Service Corps, under which the U.S. Public Health Service will provide rural and urban shortage areas with physicians, dentists, and other health personnel.

I am well aware that some of the proposals that I make in this chapter will be bitterly attacked as a deviation from "equality" of medical care. After all, is not health care a "fundamental right?" It is, but I would remind those who yearn for social utopia that medical care is a relative neophyte among fundamental rights. Far older rights are those to food, clothing, shelter, and education. Yet the poor do not enjoy the prime beef that the affluent do, and many of them must make abject confession of their poverty by lining up at public counters for food stamps. The poor do not have a choice of Sunday clothes, do not live in plush suburbs, do not send their children to uncrowded schools, or work at skilled jobs. They do not live in the mainstream, eat in the mainstream, learn in the mainstream, or work in the mainstream. The blunt, unhappy fact is that it is just not possible that they will soon swim in the mainstream of medical care. To pay lip service to mainstream medical care while many Americans are hungry and while there are neighborhoods where the few remaining doctors are afraid to venture out after dusk is to repeat the mistakes of the war on poverty. That fiasco proved rather conclusively that we are not quite ready to walk on water.

I am under no illusion that my proposals are an ideal way to treat the diseases of poverty, because they are not. What I am suggesting is only treatment of the symptoms, not the cause of the disease, a course doctors also regretfully have to follow in such other diseases as cancer, peptic ulcer, and high blood pressure. It is up to the whole American people to treat the disease of poverty itself, and it will cost billions. I hope Americans will be willing to pay that cost, and I will gladly pay my share, but let society put up or shut up. Meanwhile, let not the doctor alone be blamed for the deficiencies of health service among the poor. It would make as much sense to blame the plumber for all the stopped-up toilets in tenements.

It has been difficult for me to propose a system of health

care specifically for poor people and to suggest solutions for manpower problems that would abridge the freedom of my own profession. In the face of the hard facts, however, certain conclusions are inevitable. It would have been even more difficult for me to write with my head in the sand.

16

EVERY CHILD SHOULD BE WELCOME

My children just don't like school. They don't have fit clothing and they don't have fit shoes, and sometimes my old man doesn't bring home the money. You see, I have nine children. I have four by one man and two more by another and three by Red, the man I shack up with now. I can't find the other men. To tell you the truth, we do need food. You want me to tell you how I manage? I send Sammy, Linda, Warren and David out early every morning, and sometimes at night. These children pick up lots of food. They get it from the market stores. They pick up fire wood, too, and when they bring the stuff in, I make what I call 'a pot a day.' I'm really ashamed to tell you, but I can't well hide it. I'm caught again. I never really wanted these children. I guess that's why they're strays. All of them are strays."

A case history: Baltimore

Can any story better illustrate the dark face of poverty and the terrible problems that arise when the little money there is must be divided into ever smaller portions to feed the unwanted mouths that keep arriving? This tale is no rare instance, either. Dr. Alan F. Guttmacher of Planned Parenthood puts the number of unwanted babies born annually in the United States at 750,000. Many of these "strays" are abused or abandoned; as they grow up many turn to crime, and many require public assistance. (The poor are just as poor as they ever were, but we are improving their lot semantically. They received "charity," then "welfare," and now "public assistance.")

The vast majority of unwanted children are born to the poor. We all remember the old nursery rhyme about the old woman who lived in a shoe, who had so many children she didn't know what to do. A modern version tells about another old woman who lived in a shoe; she did not have any children; she knew what to do. The poor and the ignorant do not know what to do; the more affluent and better educated do.

I have had strong feelings about unwanted babies ever since the time, early in my medical career, when I was called to the emergency room to see a baby who had "fallen out of the high chair and don't look so good." He did not look so good because he was dead. The bruises covering his entire body indicated that he had "fallen out of the high chair" often and hard. At autopsy, the grisly findings were of many fractures, some healed and others healing. This is the battered child syndrome, the picture of a baby who has been brutally and repeatedly beaten until, in this case, bleeding from a ruptured spleen finally brought him blessed relief from torture. This same story, varying only in minor details, is sickeningly and often repeated in emergency rooms all over the country.

Family planning is one aspect of the battle against poverty that is of special interest to medicine, since it requires the services of physicians. A 1964 AMA resolution called family planning "more than a matter of reasonable parenthood; it is a matter of responsible medical practice."

The relationship between large families and poverty is undeniable. The poverty rate for families with five or six children is 350 percent higher than for families with one or two. The poor get an early start: almost 35 percent of wives from the lowest income groups are pregnant at marriage, compared to 5 percent of upper-income women. The illegitimacy rate of the poor is also far higher. Nowhere is the picture clearer than in New York, where the 12.8 percent of the population on welfare produce 50 percent of the city's babies.

Many of the poor would not be on welfare were there fewer children in the family. An income on which three or four can get by simply will not do for seven or eight. That fact lay in part behind the mail strike that spread out across the country from New York in 1970. Some of the mailmen with large families were forced to take, and were eligible for, welfare payments to supplement their U.S. Government salaries! Here is a Boston mailman described by Peter Schrag in an article entitled "Forgotten American" in *Harper's*:

A postman in a Charlestown housing project: eight children and a ninth on the way. Last year, by working overtime, his income went over $7,000. This year, because he reported it, the Housing Authority is raising his rent from $78 to $106 a month, a catastrophe for a family that pays $2.20 a day for milk, has never had a vacation and for whom an excursion is "going out for ice cream." "You try and save for something better; we hope to get out of here to some place where the kids can play, where there's no broken glass, and then something always comes along that knocks you right back. It's like being at the bottom of a well waiting for a guy to throw you a rope."

Does this forgotten American need a rope as much as his wife needs the pill?

Education, like poverty, is correlated with family size. The average number of children in American families varies from 4.7 for women with no education to 2.5 for college graduates. The figures are remarkably consistent for both whites and nonwhites. The relationship between education and family size is even more striking for Puerto Rican wives: those with no education average 6.1 children; those who have completed high school, 2.4.

The correlation was recognized by Pope Paul VI in *Humanae Vitae*: "Population growth does not seem to level off until people have achieved, through education and economic development, the skill and motivation to control the size of their families." The encyclical went on: "Stressing contraception as the answer to population problems is like putting the cart before the horse. Economic and educational development must come first."

His Holiness poses a nice problem. How can higher educational levels lower the number of births among people whose excessive births prevent better education? The fact is that the boat is taking on water faster than it is being bailed out. A drowning man does not want a swimming lesson; he needs to be saved. It would be tragic if the potential benefits of socioeconomic reforms were nullified by the problem of families too large to be properly fed, housed, and educated.

The vicious cycle of poverty must be attacked at its most vulnerable point: the large family that acts as a constant drag on the best efforts of society to reduce the size of the poverty class. Birth control is the answer to excessive fertility and the *only* answer.

The enormous benefits family planning would bring to all are obvious to anyone who has been caught in our traffic jams, who breathes our polluted air, or who has seen the asphalt spread over our green fields. But the poor are concerned less with city parks or the long lineup of autos and trailers outside Yosemite each summer day than with even more fundamental values—having enough food, clothing, and shelter to go around. It does not take a computer to figure out that on a given income there is twice as much money per person for a two-child family as there would be if there were six children. I recently saw a newspaper story that began, "Christmas will be just another day for Mrs. Irma Lee Carter and her 21 children. . . ." Another story began, "Mrs. Mary Rogers, a welfare mother, who supports her ten children on. . . ." How much better in Sweden, where birth control is universally practiced under the motto, "Every child should be welcome."

Consider this: there are at least 5 million women of childbearing age in the poverty group who need family planning services. Giving them that service would prevent the birth of 500,000 unwanted babies each year and would save the lives of 450 mothers and of 20,000 infants. At least 10,000 mentally retarded children would not be born. Such children have a life expectancy of 50 to 60 years and may cost society as much as $5000 a year to maintain.

If we spent $150 million in one year to serve the birth control needs of those 5 million women, we would save four times that much within a year in the cost of delivering their babies alone, not to mention other health-care costs. Mecklinburg County, North Carolina, found that every dollar spent on a contraceptive program saved $25 in welfare costs. On a national scale, the savings would run into the billions in a short time, money that could well be spent on ending poverty among the living. Dollars aside, what value does one place on improving the quality of life for the families not burdened with unwanted children? Although 40 percent of the poor do not use contraception, the evidence is strong that the reason is usually ignorance rather than lack of motivation. Studies have shown that the poor and uneducated do not want very large families and where family planning has been readily available to them, it has been enthusiastically accepted.

There are thousands of ways of dying, but only one way to be conceived; conception is easily and cheaply prevented. Now that the barbaric and archaic legal barriers to birth control have at last been swept aside, there still remain pockets of strong resistance, notably in the Roman Catholic Church. The church has made little progress since the police, on direct orders from Archbishop Hayes of New York, broke up the first American Birth Control Conference, organized by Margaret Sanger fifty years ago. The church no longer indicts, as it did in the past, a woman who practices unapproved birth control as accepting "the conditions of a prostitute for those of married life," but the Pope has rejected the pleas of enlightened Catholics for a modification of its ban on all methods except complete abstinence, which is unrealistic, or the rhythm method, which is unreliable. However, the official position of the church, as expressed in *Humanae Vitae*, is not accepted by many of its members. Three distinguished Catholic biologists undoubtedly spoke for many others when they said, "We are concerned about human life and human dignity, but we fail to see how the concepts expressed in (the encyclical) can lead to anything but starvation, misery, savagery and war. We find it shocking that the Pope could issue (the encyclical) against the advice of many bishops, many theologians, many laymen and especially his own birth control commission."

The practical effects of the encyclical in the United States appear to be almost nil. Some surveys have shown that a majority of Roman Catholic wives do not obey the ban, and it is likely that even these studies far understate the extent of noncompliance, since many women understandably might not want to admit it. I have conducted an analysis of several hundred Catholic women in my own practice who desire no more children; almost 100 percent of them use methods that are not sanctioned by their church. A young Catholic woman, whom I was interviewing prior to performing a vasectomy upon her husband, summed up her attitude: "If the church will assume the costs of raising and educating them, we will have more children, but so long as the financial responsibility is ours, we shall have no more."

Even less understandable than the church's rigidity in clinging to its outmoded position, however, is the opposition that comes from a few leaders of the underprivileged. Cesar Chavez, the Mexican-American leader of California farm workers, was quoted in *Time* as arguing that "smaller families would diminish the numerical power of the poor." What logic! Is poverty to be eliminated by producing more poor people? Some black militants call birth control "a white man's plot," a form of genocide aimed at wiping out the Negro race. Just as Hitler condemned birth control because he wanted cannon fodder, these misguided people are more interested in warriors ("We want black babies!") than in improving the lot of their people. Happily even black leaders acknowledge that they might be "run out of town" if they tried to keep unconvinced women out of the birth control clinics. The women who would have to bear the babies are not likely to let the politics of hate interfere with the realities of life.

Unfortunately, a good method of birth control suffered a severe setback when much of the lay press published a series of scare headlines about the pill. Senator Gaylord Nelson's 1970 hearings on the subject generated wide publicity, much of it seriously unbalanced. As a result, many women may have believed that the pill is more dangerous than is actually the case and may have given it up. One authority, Dr. Irvin M. Cushner, a Johns Hopkins University gynecologist, estimated that as many as 100,000 unwanted pregnancies might occur because frightened women had given up their pills. There is no way to check that figure, of course, but it is a fact that during the Nelson hearings Planned Parenthood offices reported that their telephone calls had doubled, with most callers seeking reassurance.

The simple fact is that the risk of the woman taking the pill is markedly less than the risk would be if she stopped it and had a child. No drug is completely without risk. Even ordinary aspirin, which we take with good effect by the billions a year, may have undesirable side effects which, on occasion, can cause a fatality. Penicillin has saved millions of lives, but it has also caused some deaths. Doctors weigh risk against potential benefit every time they prescribe a drug, and they watch carefully for unwanted effects. That is why the pill is to be taken only under medical supervision, but taken that way, it is an effective and safe method of birth control.

Much the same principles apply to the intrauterine contraceptive device (IUCD), a small bit of soft, wirelike plastic, which the doctor inserts directly into the uterus and which prevents conception in a way that we do not really understand. In a few patients it causes bleeding; a few women expel it. For the vast majority, it is harmless, effective, and, once placed in position, completely unnoticable.

For parents who have all the children they want, a still better method exists—sterilization. For the right couples, the closest thing to ideal birth control is vasectomy, sterilization of the man. The operation is safe, reliable, and permanent. It can be performed in a doctor's office in about fifteen minutes under local anesthesia. There is minimum discomfort afterward—the patient does not even have to take a day off from work. With the worry of potential pregnancy gone, most men who have had the operation report improvement in their sex lives. A survey of 1012 vasectomized Englishmen showed that 73.1 percent thought their sex was better than ever (interestingly, 79.4 percent of their wives reported improvement), and 99 percent said they would recommend the operation to others.

Sterilization of women is equally effective, but less desirable because it requires an abdominal operation in the hospital and longer recuperation, thus necessitating more pain and much higher cost. Voluntary sterilization is legal in all fifty states; in Puerto Rico "the operation" is performed more frequently than are tonsillectomies. For reasons that defy common sense, many public hospitals have the feckless rule that they will not perform the operation on a poor woman who wants it unless she has already had six or, in some cases, eight children. Why the operation should be permissible after six or eight children, when the parents are hopelessly trapped in the quagmire of poverty, but not after two or three is beyond me.

Compulsory sterilization is another matter and stirs up a heat storm whenever it is mentioned. People talk of the "constitutional and God-given right" to bring children into the world at will, even though society may have to support those children. Who speaks for the right of the child to be loved, cared for, fed, educated, and given a fair start in life? Does not the child have the right to be wanted and the right to a chance at a happy, productive life? Does this right not outweigh anyone's right to make a child an unwilling statistic on the rolls of Aid to Families with Dependent Children? These questions were raised in Nebraska in the case of a 35-year-old woman who was the mother of eight children born in a common-law relationship and who had an IQ of 71. The State Board of Examiners insisted that she remain in a state hospital until she submitted to sterilization. The Supreme Court of the state, agreeing that the woman lacked the mental stability to be a responsible parent, held, in my opinion wisely, "No citizen has any rights that are superior to the common welfare."

Having advocated what I believe to be the best form of contraception, I should also say a word about the least reliable—the rhythm method, or, as some of my Catholic friends call it, "Vatican roulette." It is true that pregnancy can be avoided by a woman sufficiently intelligent and motivated to chart her daily temperature or check the acidity and glucose content of her vaginal secretions. (The *natural* method?) Nevertheless, she must forego inter-course unnecessarily much of the time. The usual calendar method is worthless for the uneducated, and usually unmotivated, poor. We have a name for people who use the rhythm method. We call them parents. Family planning clinics should stop kowtowing to the church by offering this method to the poor. It is a cruel hoax.

Largely due to the prodding of such private organizations as Planned Parenthood, the Federal Government has lately been dipping a tentative toe into the waters of family planning. Timidity is not enough. We need an all-out national commitment to lower the fertility rate. We should open a campaign and back it up with every conceivable kind of publicity—billboards, radio and TV spots, and movie shorts. We need the same kind of national effort that we made to wipe out polio and smallpox. Poverty is an even more serious disease, and no single step could do more to alleviate it than a vigorous family planning program. Fortunately, a national program would not have to start from scratch. Thanks to the vision of Dr. Alan F. Guttmacher and other pioneers of Planned Parenthood, a large corps of knowledgeable people have been trained to conduct family planning clinics. The vanguard for the campaign is already there.

Though I am more concerned about McDowell County, West Virginia, than Westchester County, New York, family planning, of course, should not be confined to the poor. Anyone who contributes to the population explosion is harming society. In this respect our income tax laws are totally wrong, encouraging large families as they do by granting exemptions for each child born. The law needs to be reversed; it should penalize large families.

I am not like some of the timid souls in Washington who

are worried about coercing people into family planning. I would pull out all stops in the attempt to break the cycle of poverty. By all means let us persuade, urge, and advise people, but if in the end we have to coerce some people, so be it. Poverty is a serious disease and needs the strongest control measures. In other fields we do not hesitate to coerce a few people in order to assure the rights of many. There can be no more precious human right than the right of a child to be welcome.

17

"THOU SHALT NOT KILL"

PROBABLY the most widely used method of birth control is abortion. Nobody really knows how many abortions are being performed. Some estimates run as high as 25 million annually worldwide of which a million a year are performed illegally in the United States. Illegal abortions, almost always performed under less than optimum conditions and often under unspeakable conditions, can be killers; complications resulting from illegal abortions are the second commonest cause of maternal mortality.

Most abortions are not performed upon light ladies seeking to escape the penalties of dalliance, but upon married women who have had several children and want no more. The more children, the more likely an abortion. About one-third of all pregnancies of women who have already had five children are terminated by abortion. Despite the absolute ban of the Catholic Church, religion appears to be no barrier. In Catholic South America, the abortion rate is at least double that in the United States. In Uruguay there are as many induced abortions as there are live births.

Insofar as the law is concerned, in the United States at

the moment all is confusion. A number of states have recently liberalized their abortion laws; as I write, bills to accomplish that end are pending in the legislatures of others. In several jurisdictions, abortion is available on demand, or practically so; for example, New York, where the country's most liberal law by far became effective July 1, 1970, and Wisconsin and the District of Columbia, where the courts have thrown out old laws and no new ones at all presently exist to replace them. The issue comes before the U.S. Supreme Court during its 1970–71 term, and it is possible that many or all abortion prohibitions could be held unconstitutional.

In some states where laws have already been liberalized, there is confusion. In California a woman's chances of obtaining a legal abortion may vary with her location. Around San Francisco, there is a more progressive attitude about abortions than in the Los Angeles area, although southern Californians are just catching up with the more liberal northerners. The question of whether she has money is also important; a private patient has at least double the chance of obtaining an abortion as does a Medicaid patient. At any rate, the new liberalized law in California is having a dramatic effect. Only 5000 legal abortions were performed in 1968, the first year of the new law; in 1970 the number rose to 70,000.

The patient with money, no matter where she lives, can have a legal abortion in New York. I have just received a letter, presumably sent to practicing physicians all over the country, inviting me to refer patients to New York's Park East Hospital. The hospital's services, including anaesthetist and a 24-hour stay, cost $325, with any extra stay, if required, at no extra charge. The doctor's fee, says the hospital, is $250, so for $575, plus the price of a plane ticket, the lady's problem is solved. Poor residents of New York may be aborted without charge in the public hospitals, though there may be a waiting list, and certainly there is less luxury.

No matter what happens to our laws in the immediate future, the arguments over abortion are certain to continue, and with heat. No quarrel is more charged with emotion on both sides. Some of the so-called medical arguments against abortion are simply folklore; both the dangers of the procedure and its sequelae have been grossly exaggerated. Mortality and morbidity are extremely low when the operation is performed by a qualified person under aseptic conditions in a hospital or a properly equipped clinic. It is at least five times as dangerous for a woman to continue the pregnancy to term. Psychiatric aftereffects are far less common after abortion than after childbirth. The claim that a liberal abortion policy will lead to promiscuity holds no water. It has not happened in countries where laws have been liberalized. If that were a valid objection to abortion, it would certainly be even more valid when applied to contraception, but few would go back to outlawing that.

The only real issue was stated by Dr. James McNulty, a former member of the California State Board of Medical Examiners: "The fertilized egg is either a blob of protoplasm or else it is a human being endowed with all the rights and privileges guaranteed by the Constitution." Quite so. If it is indeed a human being, then, as opponents of abortion claim, abortion is "a kind of lynching in the womb"; it is murder—a violation of the fifth commandment, "Thou shalt not kill."

If that egg is "just a blob of protoplasm," then abortion is in the realm of private morality. *Under these circumstances* a woman has just as much right to rid herself of that egg, which she and her physician consider harmful to her health, as they would have to remove a cancerous tumor on the same ground. No one has the right to dictate another's morality, whether the issue be eating meat on Friday, keeping a kosher kitchen, or removing tissue from the uterus.

A fetus is either viable or not viable, and there is no halfway state. The moment it is outside the mother's body and living, it is an infant. Only on the rarest of occasions can it become an infant and maintain an independent existence prior to 26 weeks of gestation. If pregnancy is terminated prior to this time, the result is a nonviable fetus weighing a pound or less. If that happens without assistance, the event is called spontaneous abortion or miscarriage, and the fetus is not listed in the vital statistics as a newborn infant. There is no funeral. The fetus is disposed of by the hospital pathologist, just as he would dispose of, say, an appendix that had been removed. Should a fetus be shot or stabbed in utero during the first 26 weeks of pregnancy and pregnancy terminated, the assailant is not charged with homicide. Legally, homicide is not committed until after the fetus is viable.

From these considerations I reason that up to the 26th week of pregnancy, the fetus is nonviable, and therefore I see no valid moral or medical objections to removing it. I would consider it murder to remove and destroy the fetus during the last three months of pregnancy. Abortion prior to that time is none of the law's business. It is a matter of private, rather than public, morality to be settled between the woman and her physician.

At a 1967 International Conference on Abortion, Mrs. Sargent Shriver raised the private versus public question: "Should mothers be permitted to make their decisions solely on the basis of their own personal, individualistic, private desires, or should someone speak on these matters for society as a whole for ethical and religious principles?" But she herself had answered this question two years earlier in an article in *Mc Call's* extolling the virtues of the large family: "The decision to have children is the most delicate and intimate—and certainly the most important —decision that can be made in a marriage. It should be a generous and a *private choice*, untouched by feelings of guilt" (italics mine).

The philosophy of a private choice should—but doubtless will not—please everybody. The woman who has no qualms about abortion would prevent the birth of an unwanted child and feel the happier for it. The woman who disagrees could also act according to her conscience and go through with pregnancy, even if it be due to rape or if the fetus is horribly deformed. Those who feel that every pregnancy is "an act of God" (even when conception took place because two teenagers in the rear seat of a car depended upon Saran Wrap and a Coca-Cola douche to prevent conception) should certainly not resort to a practice which in their eyes is tantamount to murder. In actual practice, however, I have found that the most pure of hearts tends to change his attitude when his own 15-year-old daughter tearfully announces that she has been "blessed."

18

THE COURT OF LAST RESORT

I have attempted in these pages to establish the causes of medicine's most serious ills and to offer prescriptions for their cures. There is no dispute that our health-care system is in deep trouble because of manpower shortages, uneven quality of care, and steeply rising costs. We have the knowledge, the ability, and the resources to solve these problems, but medicine is not an island unto itself. Health needs must compete for dollars and personnel with the urgent tasks of eliminating poverty, rejuvenating our inner cities, purifying our polluted environment, and providing better education for the disadvantaged. Obviously there is no cheap and quick solution to our health problems. It will take a major national commitment and a long period of time before we approach utopia.

Meanwhile there is much that we can do with our present resources. Of all the ingredients necessary to alleviate our most pressing problem, the shortage of doctors, only two are missing. We have the know-how, the bricks, the mortar, and the all-important candidates for admission to medical schools. All that is lacking is the will and the money. The will must be strong enough to move the Federal Government, since only Washington can supply the money.

Giving the doctor more assistance will help, but the answer does not lie in a new category of physician's assistants who would be acceptable to neither doctor nor patient, except possibly in remote locations or other situations where no other solution can be found. Nurses, technicians, and ancillary help of all kinds are also scarce and very badly needed. Schools to train them are already in existence and have established legal status and well-defined objectives. It would be far better to upgrade the responsibility of the nurse and other technicians than to interpose new health workers between the doctor and his time-honored assistants.

We may also find that raising the quality of care will also help mitigate the manpower shortage. Useless operations that place unnecessary burdens upon scarce hospital beds and personnel easily can be regulated out of existence. Even more important, strict controls over the quality of care will reduce needless suffering, sometimes even needless deaths. And, paradoxical as it may seem, improving quality should even lower costs. The matter of relieving the suffering of the medically unsophisticated is too important to be left to what organized medicine likes to call "individual judgment" and "peer review." Medicine's record for self-regulation has differed little from that of the military investigating the military-industrial complex or from labor unions controlling probes of labor unions. The name of that game is whitewash.

Such measures will help to brake the escalating cost of care, but can do no more than that. Inflation generally, increasing labor costs in hospitals specifically, and the continuing development of new and miraculous, but expensive, forms of treatment insure that costs will keep spiraling upward. We cannot let a spell of ill health constitute a disaster to a man and his family any more than a fire or automobile accident should, and the answer to these problems is the same: insurance. Although national health insurance, by spreading risk and allowing budgetling, is essential, it will produce chaos without stricter controls on the quality of care and the production of enough doctors to deliver that care. Medicare and Medicaid have amply demonstrated the dangers of simply pumping more money into a system that is not able to do the job. If demand and ability to pay rise while supply does not, inflation of prices can be the only result. War plans are no good without the guns and manpower to put them into effect.

Nor can we solve our problems by blowing up our medical schools, as a few simplistic and nihilistic students suggest. Unlike our health statistics, our medical schools are the envy of the rest of the world. It is not the job of medical schools to turn out urban planners, anthropologists, or sociologists. There are other schools for that. The medical school is the place to turn out *doctors*, men and women who help, *one by one*, people who are troubled by ulcers, gallstones, diabetes, sexual impotence, or heart trouble. It is also a starting point for public health physicians, those who are interested in preserving community health, rather than in curing individuals. Sanitation engineers can help thousands by exterminating rats, cleaning up garbage, and removing lead paint from the walls of slum apartments. Medicine, sociology, and sanitation engineering are all respected professions, but it is a rare genius who can perform respectably at all three. By all means, the personal physician should be concerned about general social problems and should do his part to solve them, but it is not clear to me that he should neglect his primary duty in order to do so.

Sick patients are interested most of all in getting well. Helping them is the doctor's job. That is why I do not expect that medical schools and legislatures will succeed in turning out more "family physicians" and fewer specialists. Sick people want the best doctors they can get, and medical students want to be the best doctors they can be. It is true that some specialists have tunnel vision and are interested only in what they can see through an otoscope or a vaginal speculum, but that is not true of most of us. Professional competence and compassion are not incompatible.

We live in a pluralistic society, and I advocate a pluralistic health-care delivery system. I have no quarrel with prepaid group practice; some plans, certainly not all, are performing very well indeed. But this is not a panacea for *all* patients and *all* doctors. Any attempt from Washington to force everybody into this Procrustean bed can end only in disaster. Each generation in medicine has built upon the accomplishments of its forebears. There is much that is good in today's medical structure, and we must hold on to it, even in the Age of Aquarius. Pluralism is the key: the doctor must be able to choose the way of practice that suits him best, and so must the patient.

The medical care needs of the poor is an especially thorny issue and some seem to think all their health problems can be solved by neighborhood health centers, like those currently financed by the Federal Government through the OEO. These centers are necessary and desirable in our present parlous situation, but they should be satellites of the local city or county hospital's outpatient departments in order to have the full back-up they require. I see nothing in a health bureaucracy with a Washington zip code number that will enable it to outperform a bureaucracy headquartered in City Hall. The disgraceful deterioration of our public hospitals in recent years has been partly due to the shortage of doctors and ancillary personnel, but far more to the fact that local governments have been starving them for money.

Telling the poor that it is their right to enter the mainstream of medical care may do wonders for the careers of some political opportunists, but it will not help the poor unless we have the facilities for them to use. The poor know, very well indeed, what their health needs are, but they do not have the professional capacity to provide for them, and it hardly helps to have a bunch of self-styled community leaders, engaged in vicious infighting for political power, pummeling the professionals who are the only people who can do the job. Such slogans as "All power to the people" sound great, but they do not cure diabetes.

We should seek to provide one level of health care for everybody, regardless of ability to pay. But harsh reality makes clear that this will not happen overnight. Whether we like it or not, the poor and the affluent eat differently, are housed differently, are educated differently. The black tenant farmer in Mississippi and the *chicano* in California do not—and for the foreseeable future cannot—live like the bank president in Scarsdale. Just as public housing (also far from ideal) has been found necessary to deal with slum living, so will public hospitals be necessary to meet today's health needs of the poor. I am not proposing two standards of medical care quality; I have made plain that our public hospitals can and often do maintain higher *quality standards* than do many private hospitals, even though they cannot provide the luxuries. What I do want to argue, with all the force that I can muster, is that we must give them the money necessary to enable them to do their job. But as long as poverty is a major problem in this country, the medical needs of the poor will largely be provided in a different setting from that of the more affluent. When we rid ourselves of hungry children, slum hosuing, and third-rate education, we shall be ready to rid this country of public hospitals—and not before.

Being no sociologist, politician, or militant, but only a doctor, I offer few suggestions for alleviating the plight of the poor. I do know, however, that the limitation of family size is of paramount importance in breaking the vicious cycle of generation-to-generation poverty. Family planning is as necessary in the city slums and rural poverty pockets of the United States as it is in the miserable *barriadas* of Peru, and legalized abortion is an integral part of population control the world over. If the birth rate in this country were lowered to that of the other advanced countries, training midwives to deliver babies would not be necessary and our high infant mortality rate would decrease.

In this book I have washed some of my own profession's dirty linen in medicine's troubled waters. Some of my colleagues will consider this the unforgivable sin: Hippocrates admonished us that should a physician witness "deleterious and mischievous" practices, he must "not divulge, as reckoning that all such should be kept secret."

If I have sinned, so be it. To my mind nefarious medical practices must not be kept secret, nor can we neglect the deficiencies in our present health care. I am constitutionally unable to sweep problems under the carpet.

Although I have been strident in calling public attention to bad medical care, I have tried to be moderate in prescribing solutions. I have seen far more despicable medical practices than those I have described in this book, but my purpose has not been to tell a series of horror stories. It is enough to establish the fact that we do tolerate substandard health practices in this country and that we can and must improve our medical care. My intention has not been simply to irritate my medical colleagues, but to jolt them into action. I continue to see people maimed and exploited at fully accredited hospitals where I would not take a sick dog. Organized medicine is unwilling to cope with these abuses, government agencies are powerless to cope with them, and the insurance carriers who control the purse strings disdain to cope with them.

How long can one remain silent and watch the cruel, unnecessary loss of life and limb? Perhaps if I were a young militant, I would throw rocks and eventually bombs through the windows of HEW and the AMA. Instead, I appeal to the court of last resort—the American public.

APPENDIX OF ABBREVIATIONS

Government Agencies with Important Health Functions

FDA   Federal Drug Administration
HEW   Department of Health, Education and Welfare
NIH   National Institutes of Health
OEO   Office of Economic Opportunity
RMP   Regional Medical Programs
SSA   Social Security Administration
USPHS   United States Public Health Service
VA   Veterans Administration

Health Organizations

AAMC   American Association of Medical Clinics
AAMC   American Association of Medical Colleges
AHA   American Hospital Association
AMA   American Medical Association
ANA   American Nursing Association
JCAH   Joint Commission on Accreditation of Hospitals
NMA   National Medical Association

Professional Organizations

AAGP   American Academy of General Practice
AAP   American Academy of Pediatrics

ACOG American College of Obstetrics and Gynecology
ACP American College of Physicians
ACS American College of Surgeons

APPROVED SPECIALTY BOARDS

American Board of Anesthesiology
American Board of Colon and Rectal Surgery
American Board of Dermatology
American Board of Family Practice
American Board of Internal Medicine
American Board of Neurological Surgery
American Board of Obstetrics and Gynecology
American Board of Ophthalmology
American Board of Orthopaedic Surgery
American Board of Otolaryngology
American Board of Pathology
American Board of Pediatrics
American Board of Physical Medicine and Rehabilitation
American Board of Plastic Surgery
American Board of Preventive Medicine
American Board of Psychiatry and Neurology
American Board of Radiology
American Board of Surgery
American Board of Urology
Board of Thoracic Surgery